I0481176

Calligraphy Practice Book

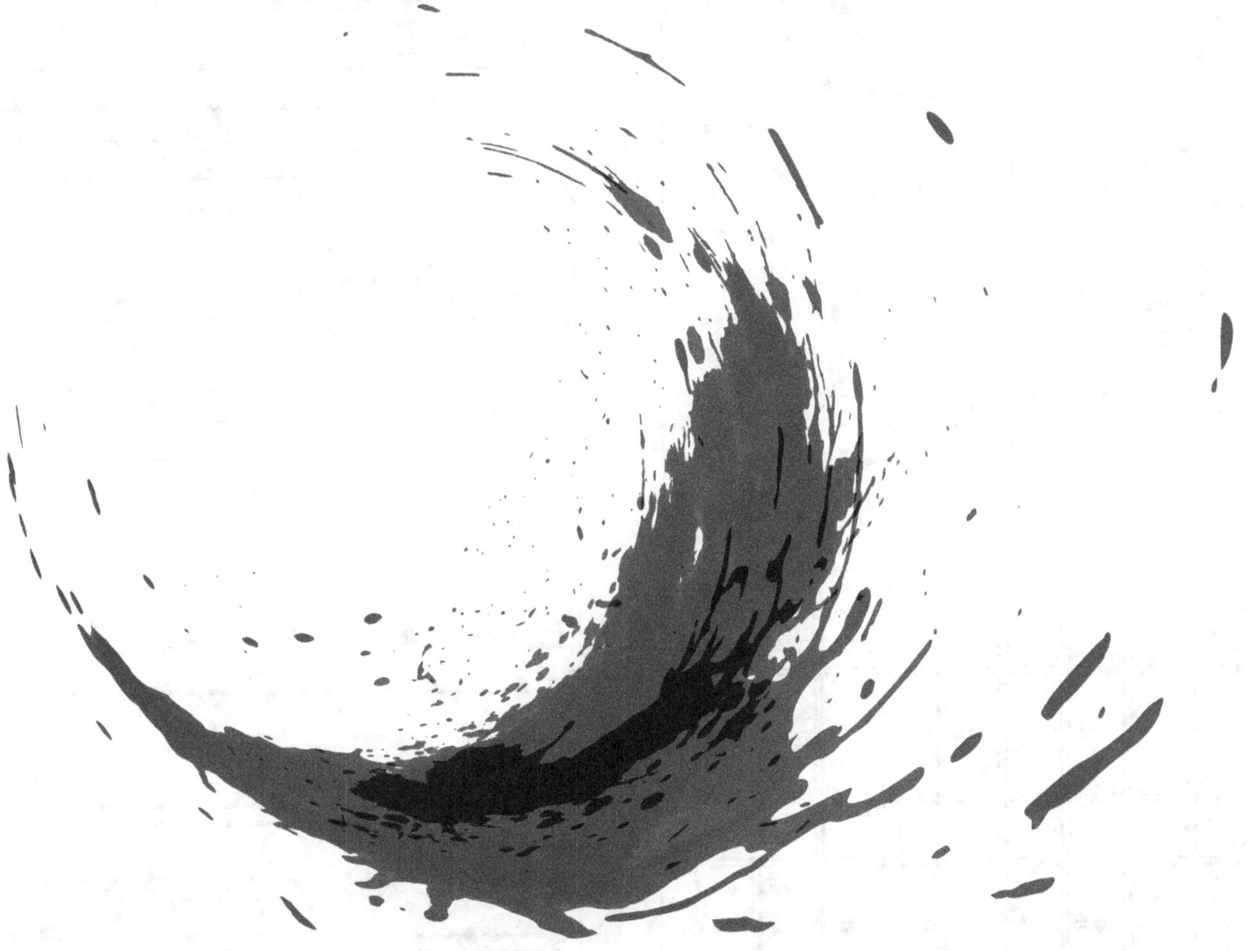

Copyright © 2017
ISBN-13: 978-1981837847
ISBN-10: 1981837841

Example

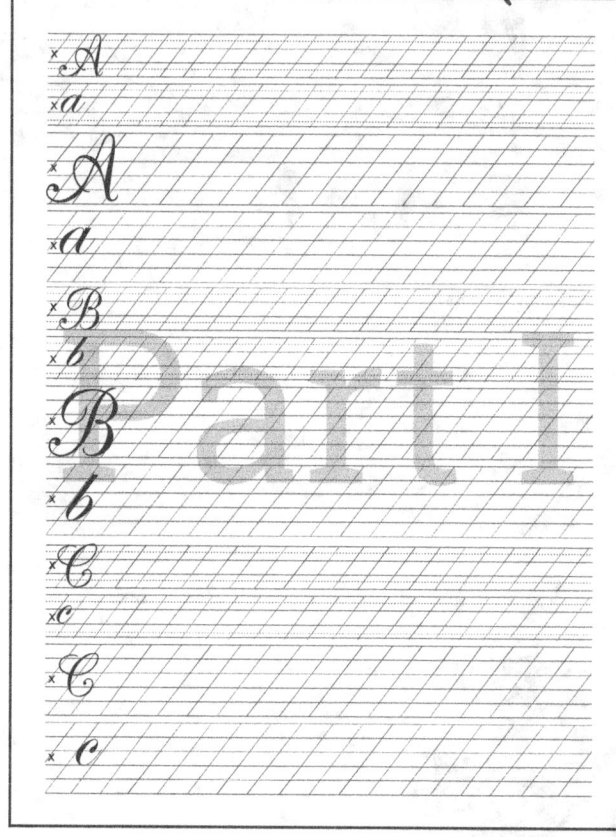

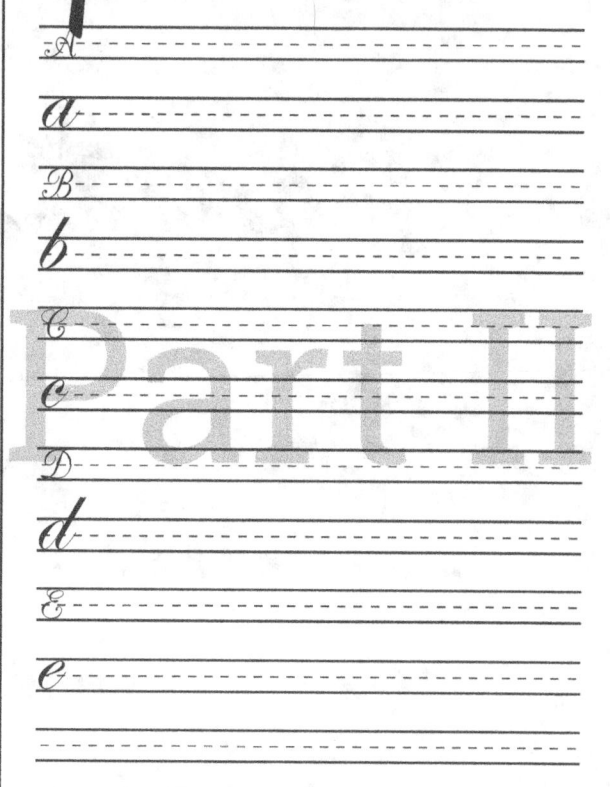

DUAL BRUSH PENS

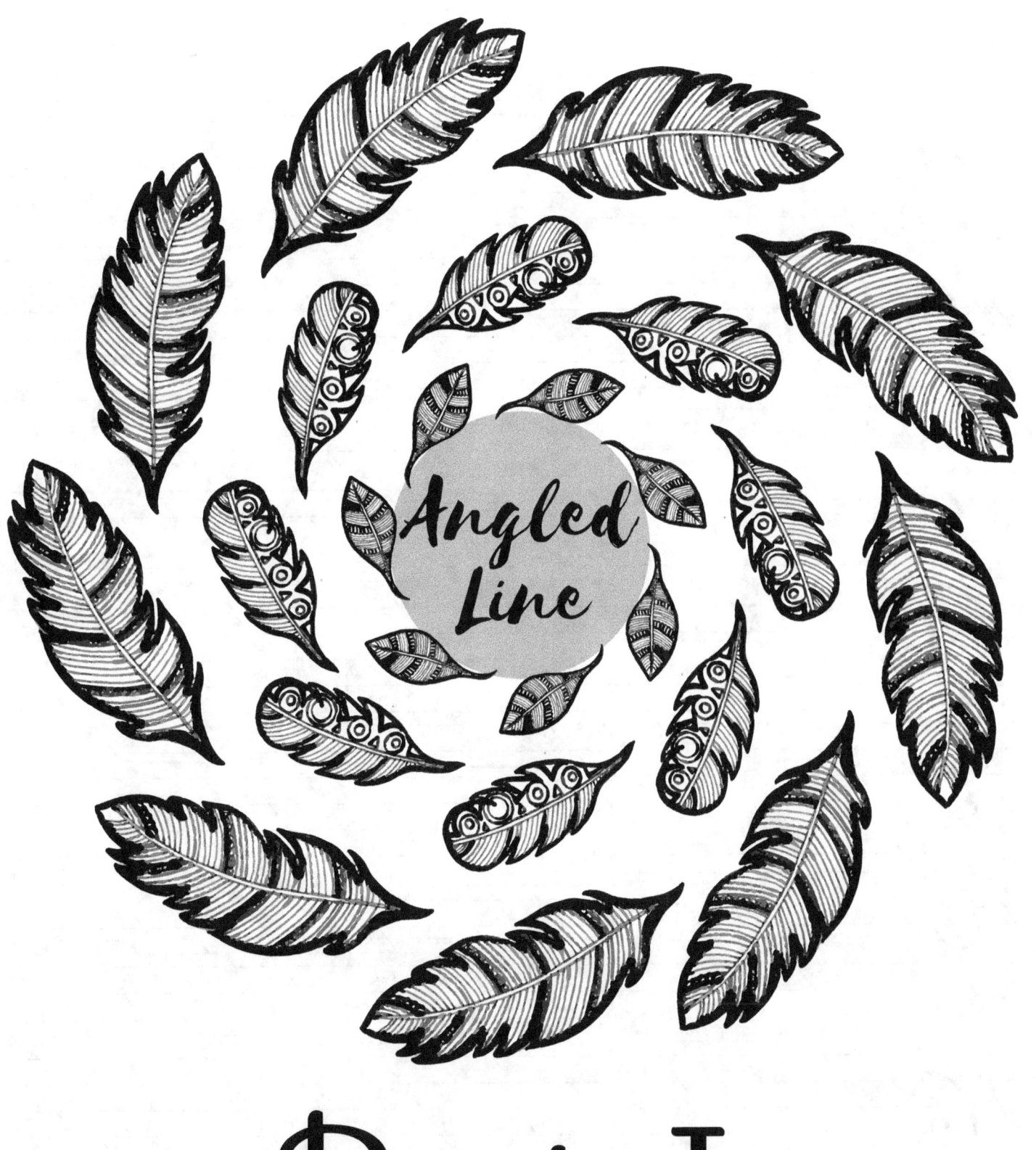

Angled Line

Part I

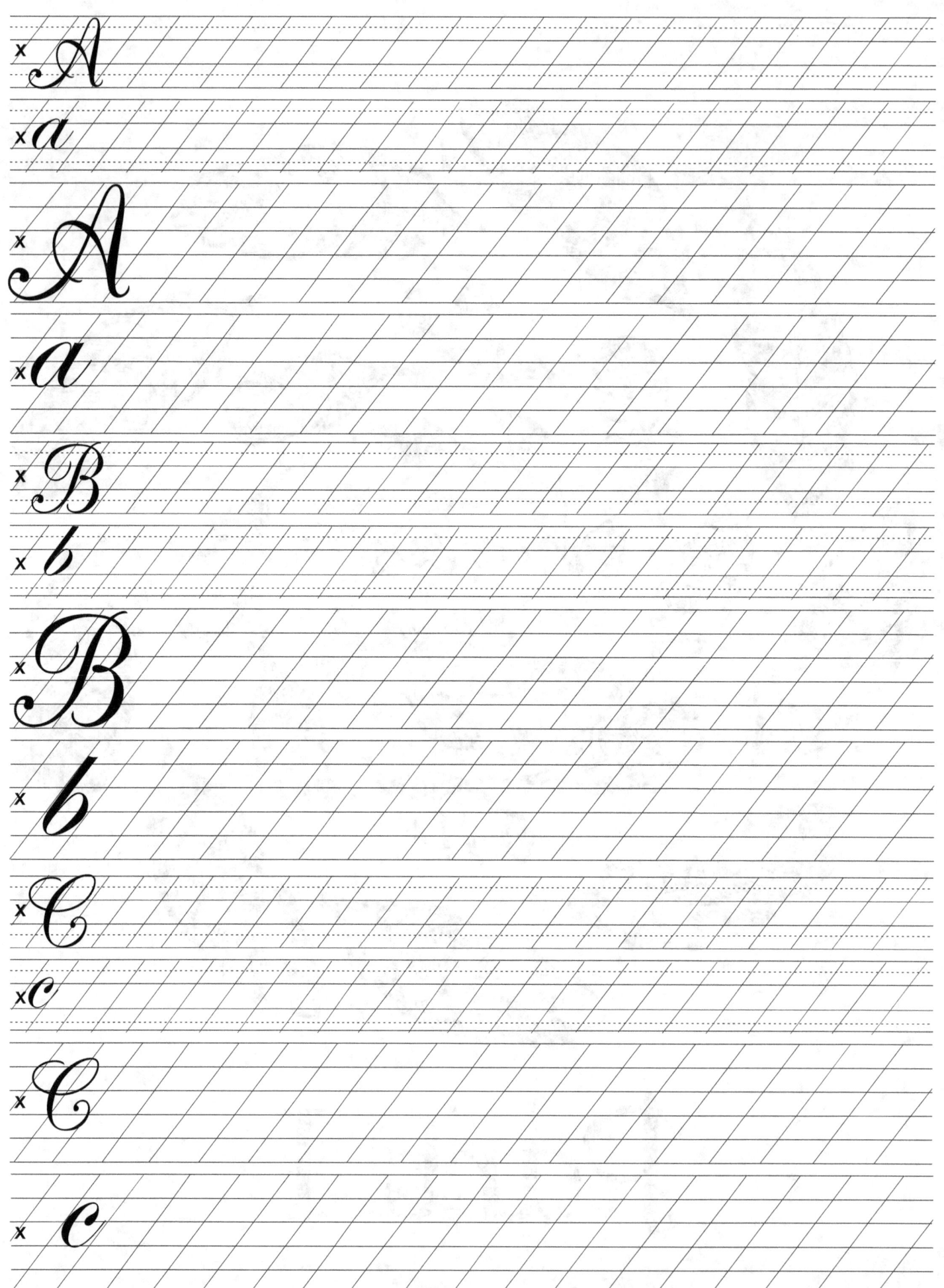

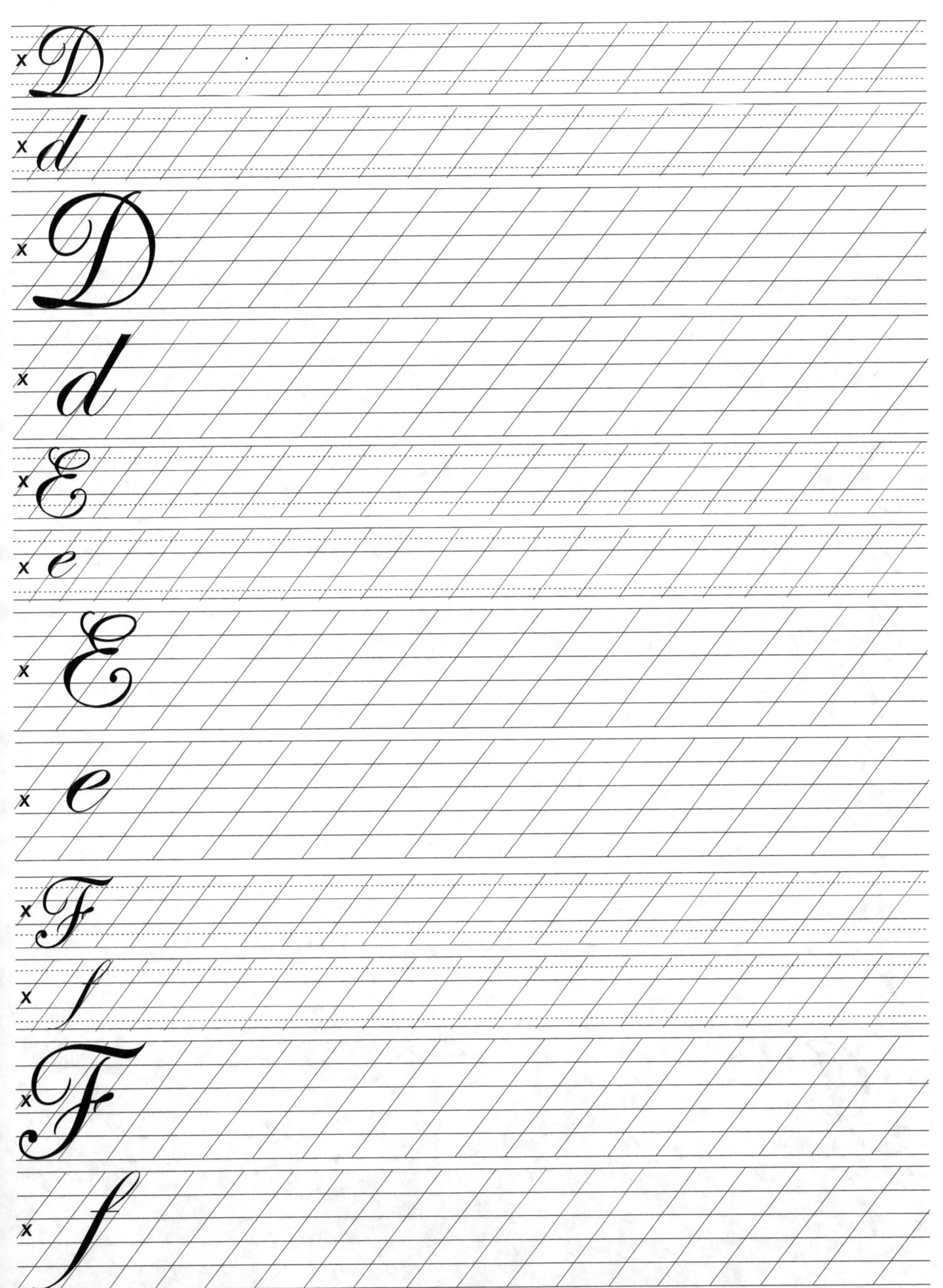

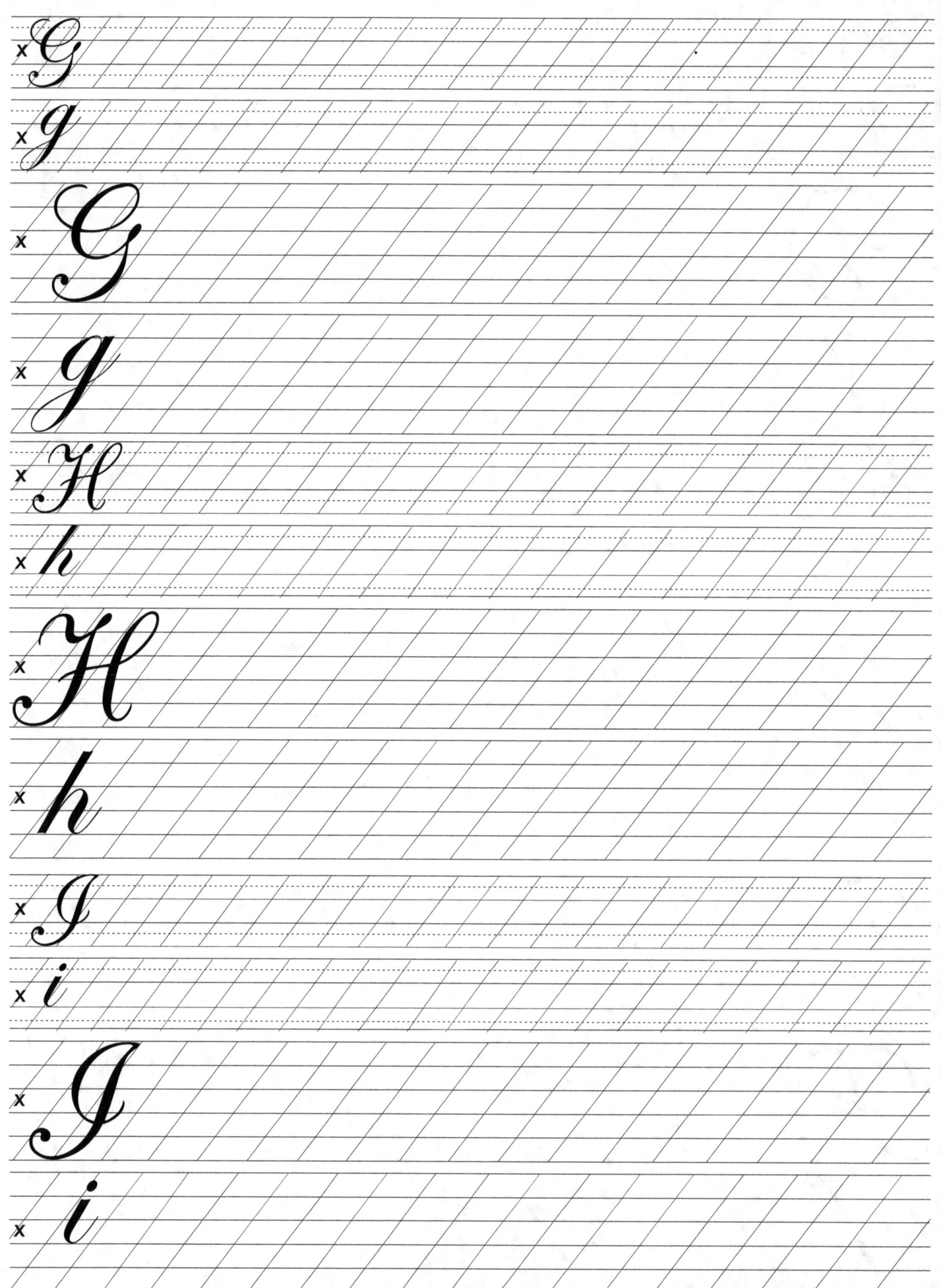

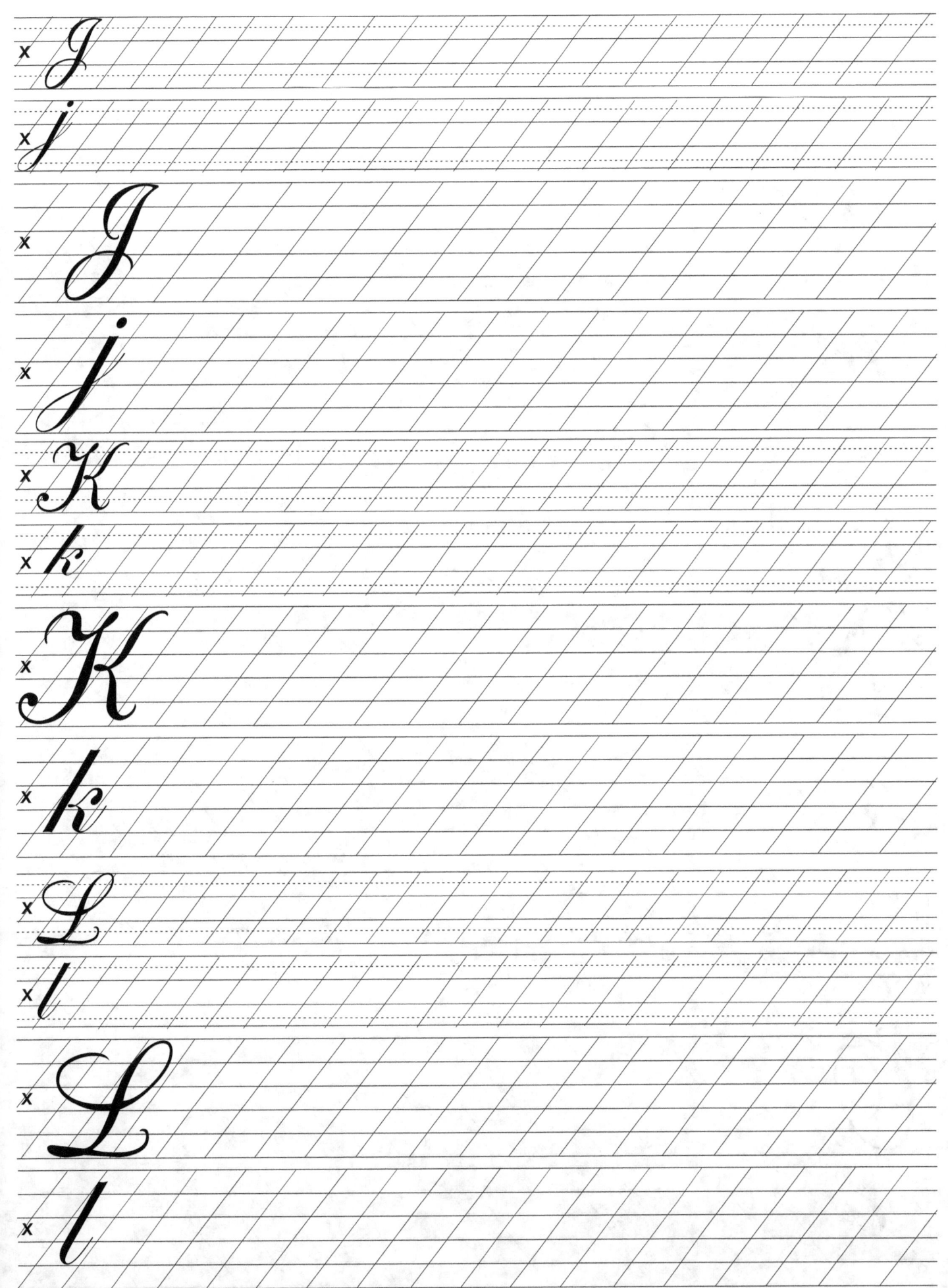

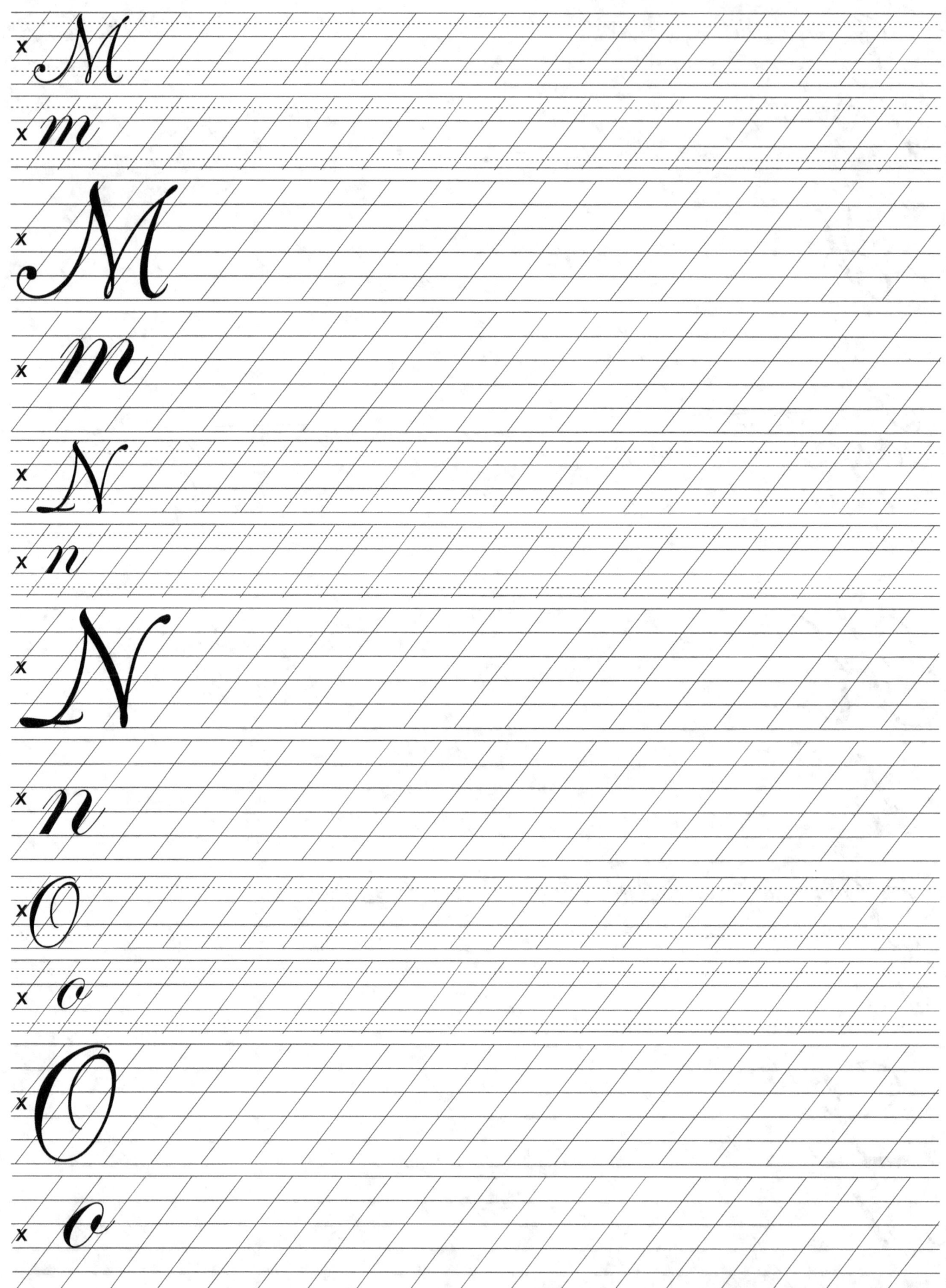

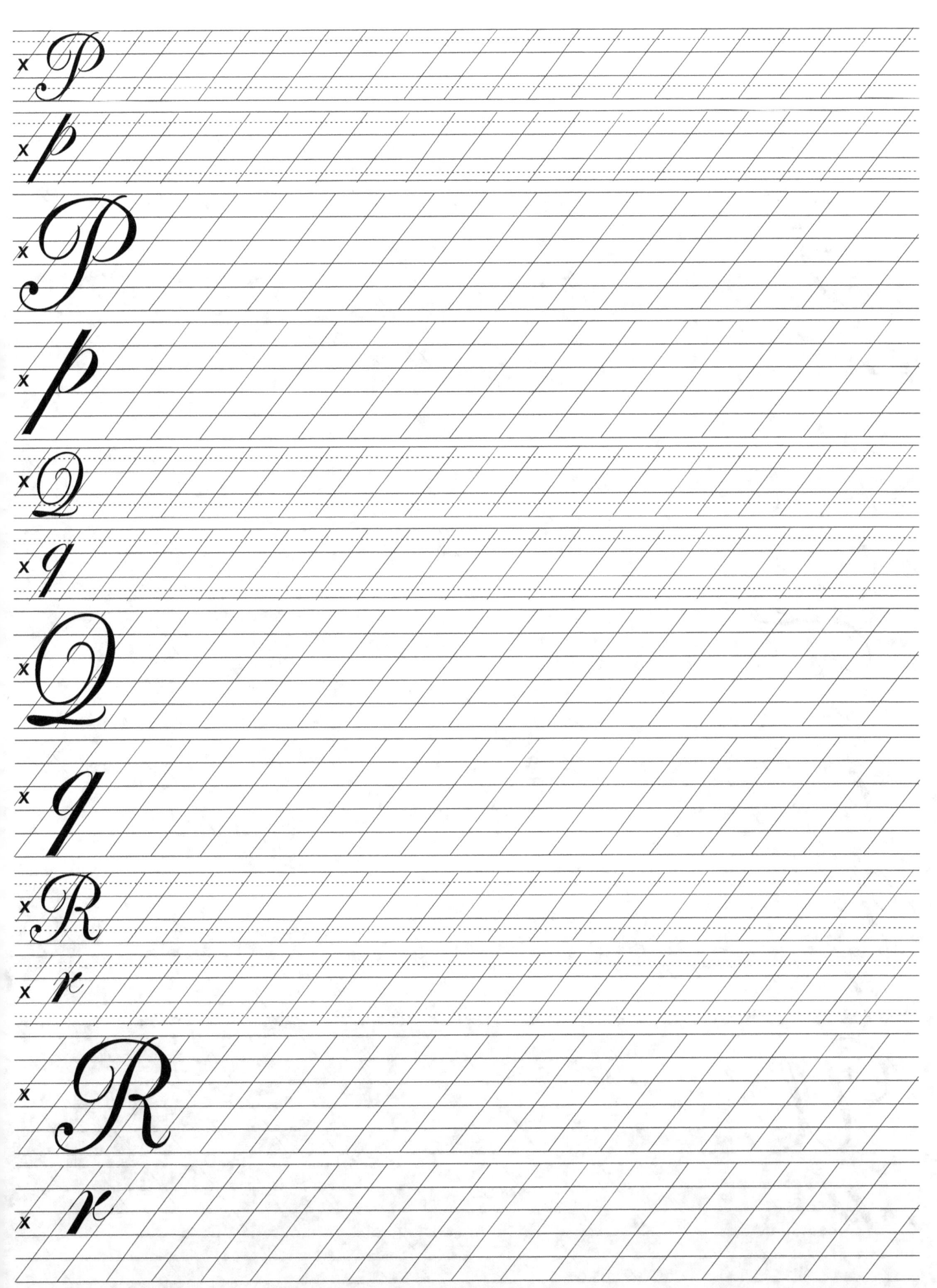

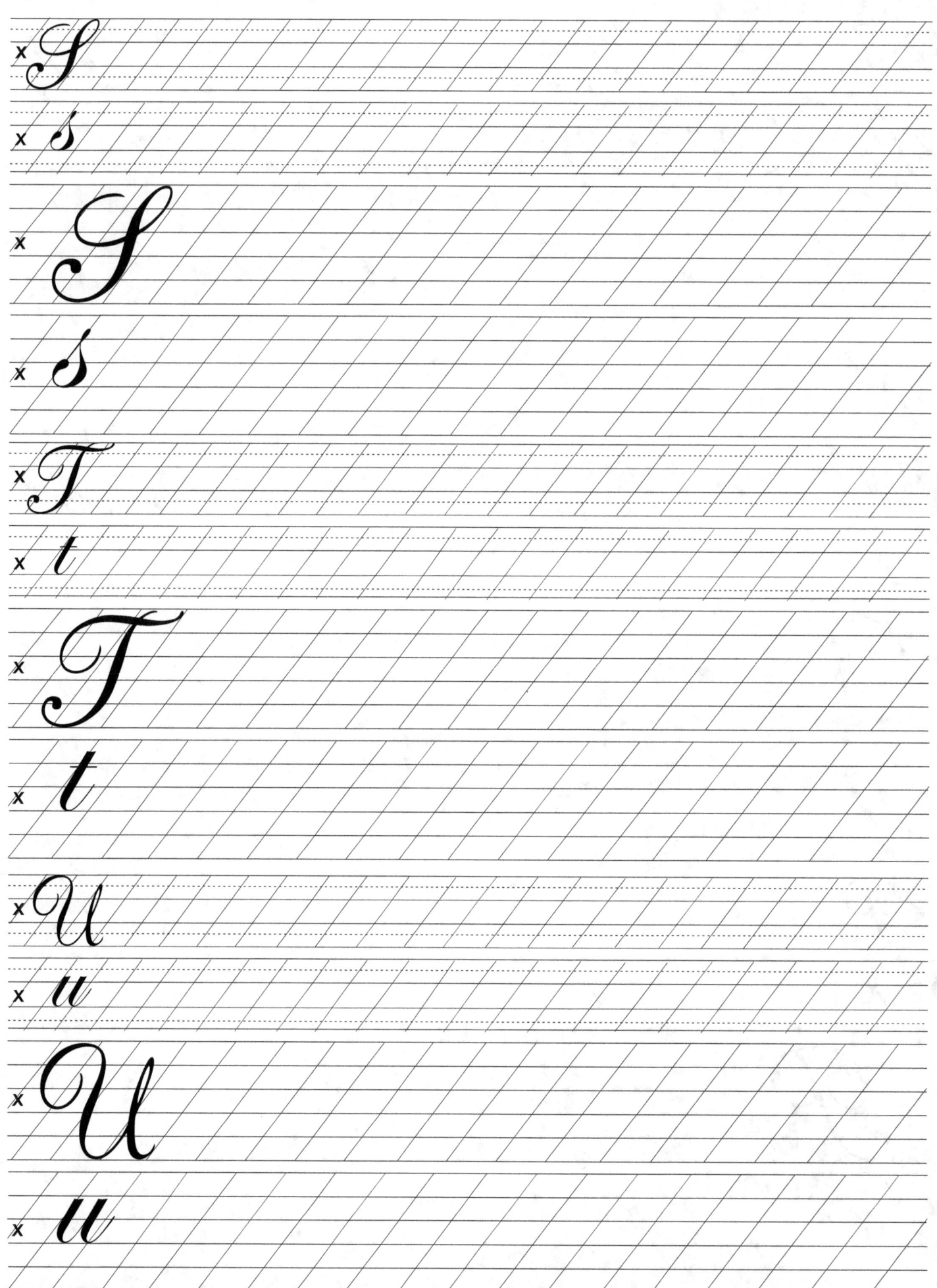

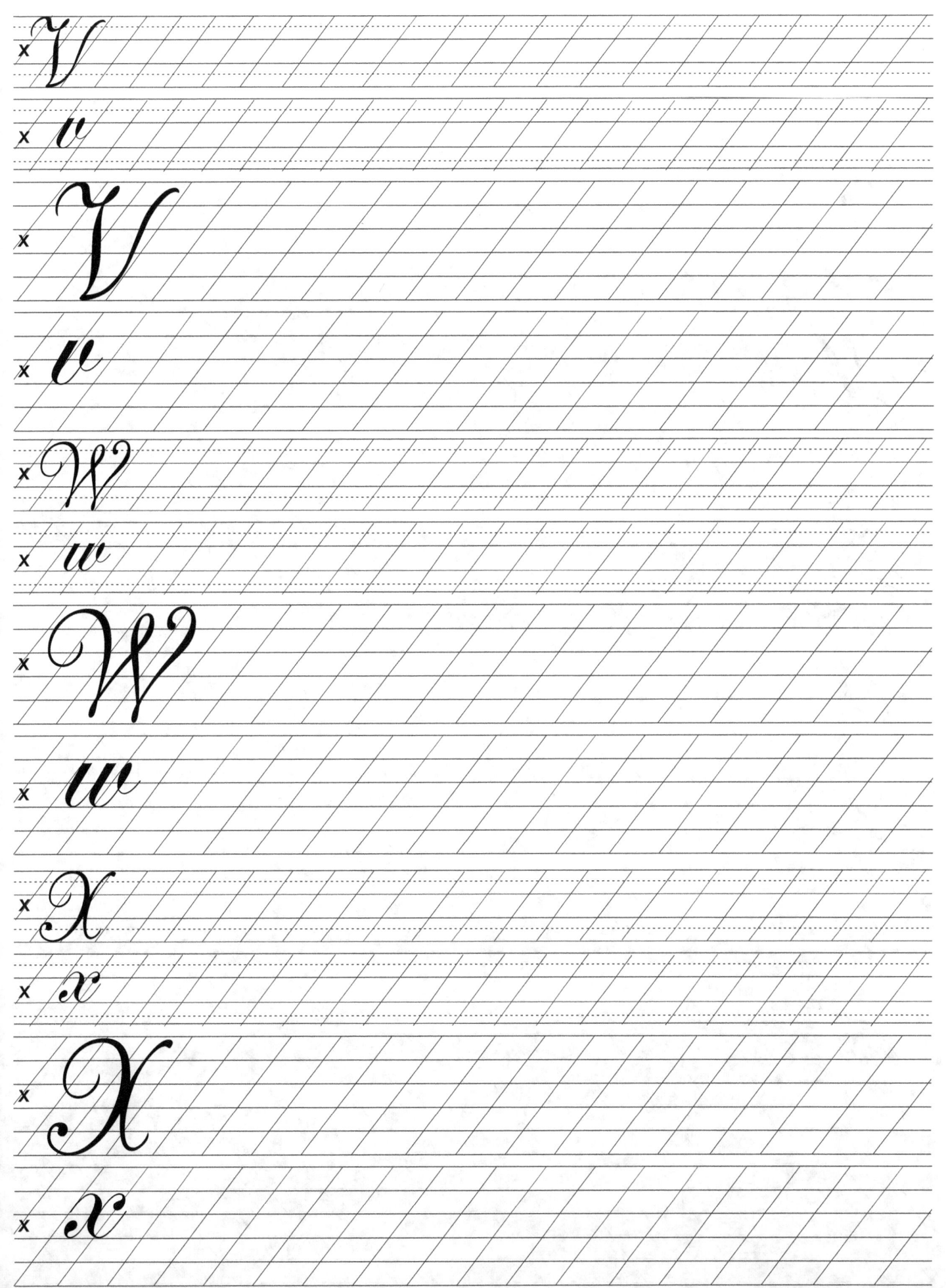

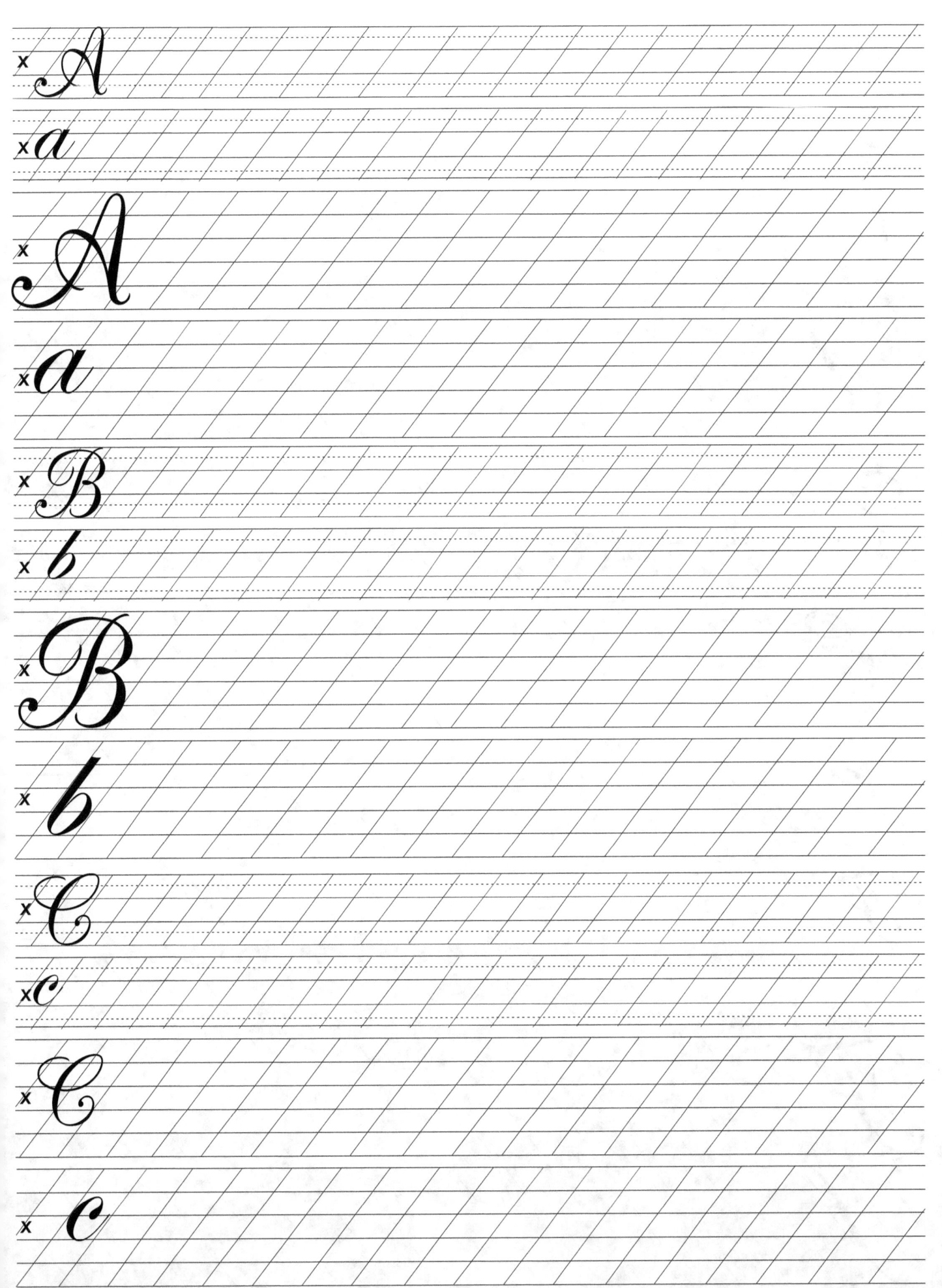

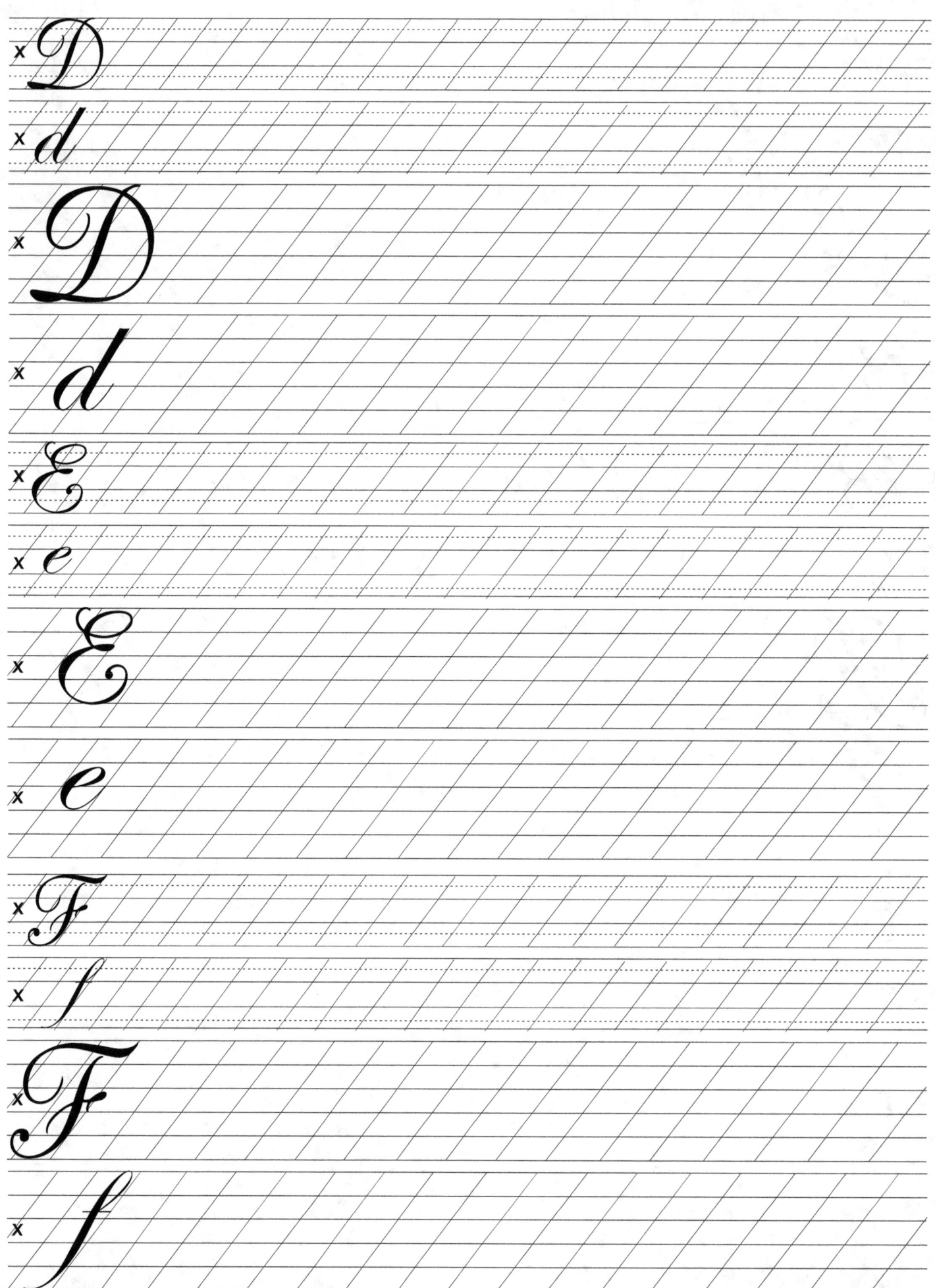

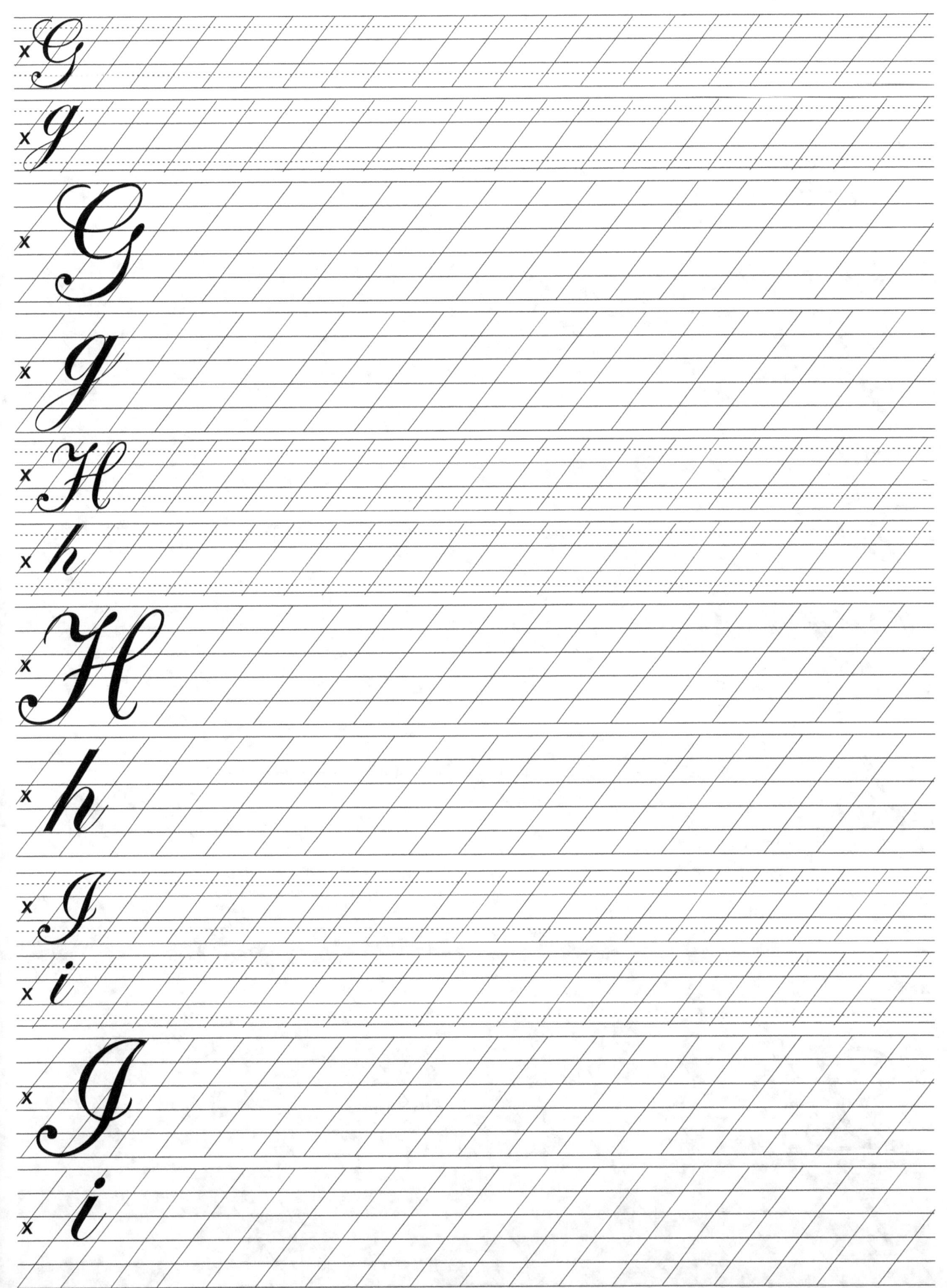

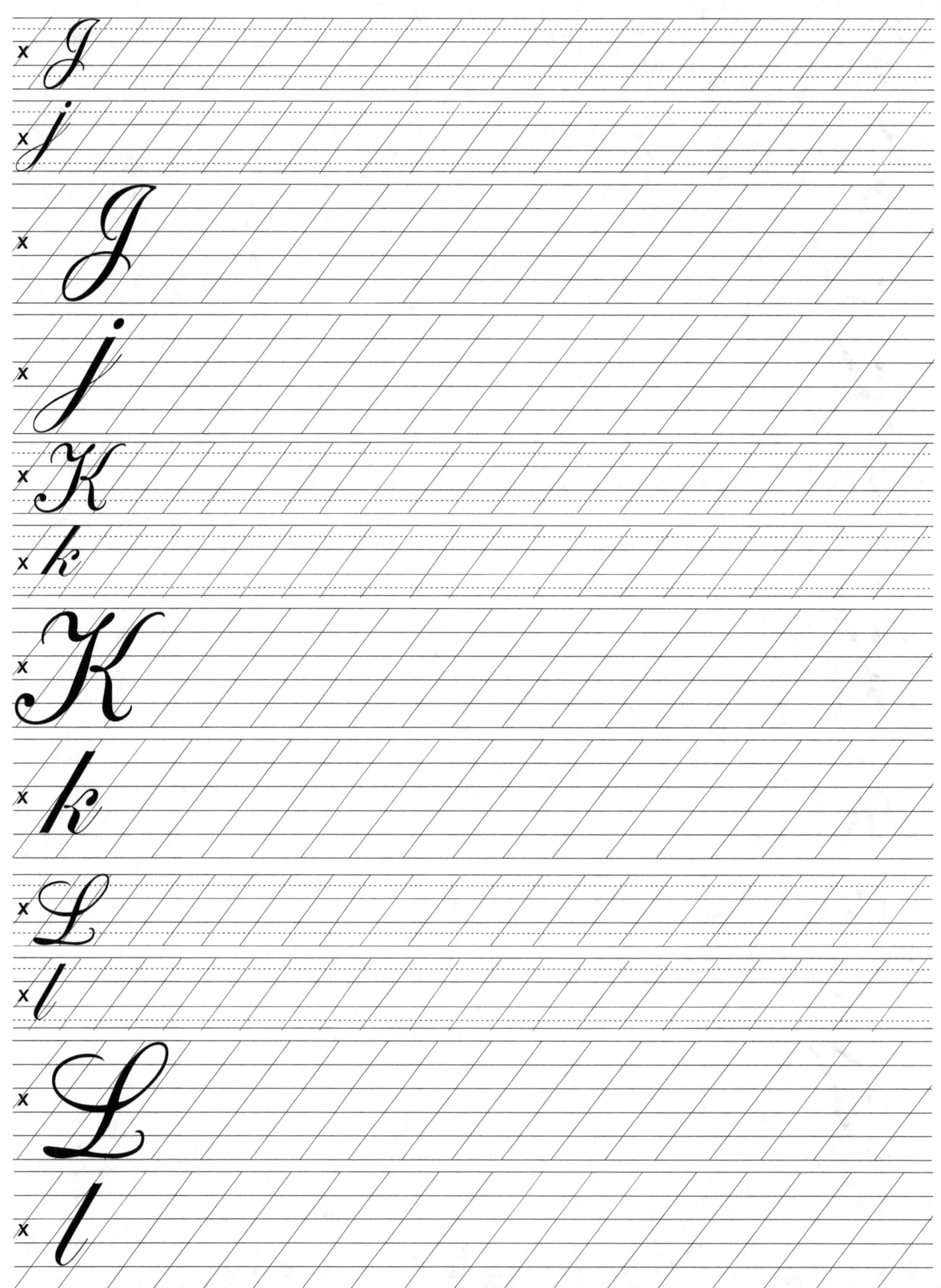

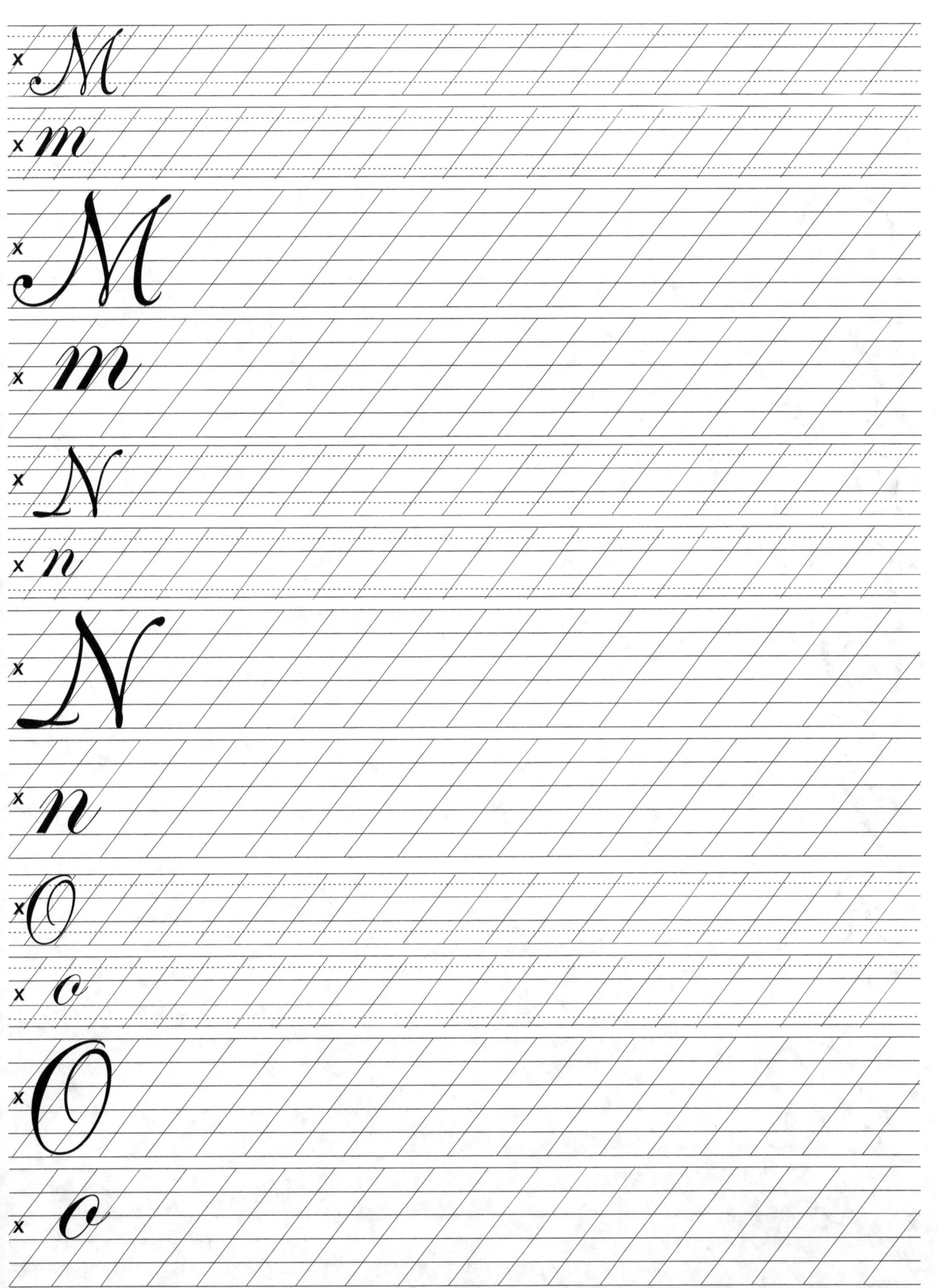

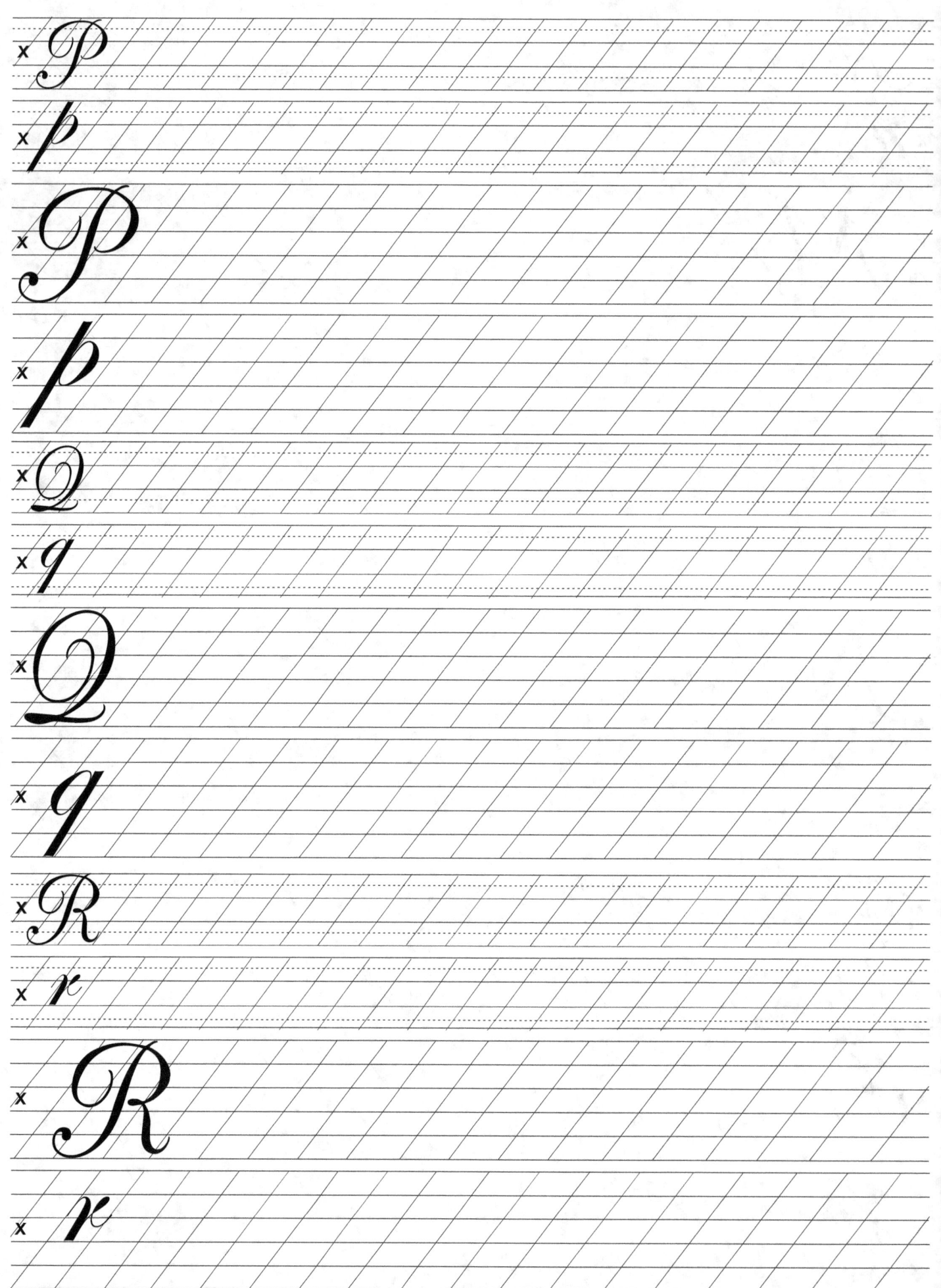

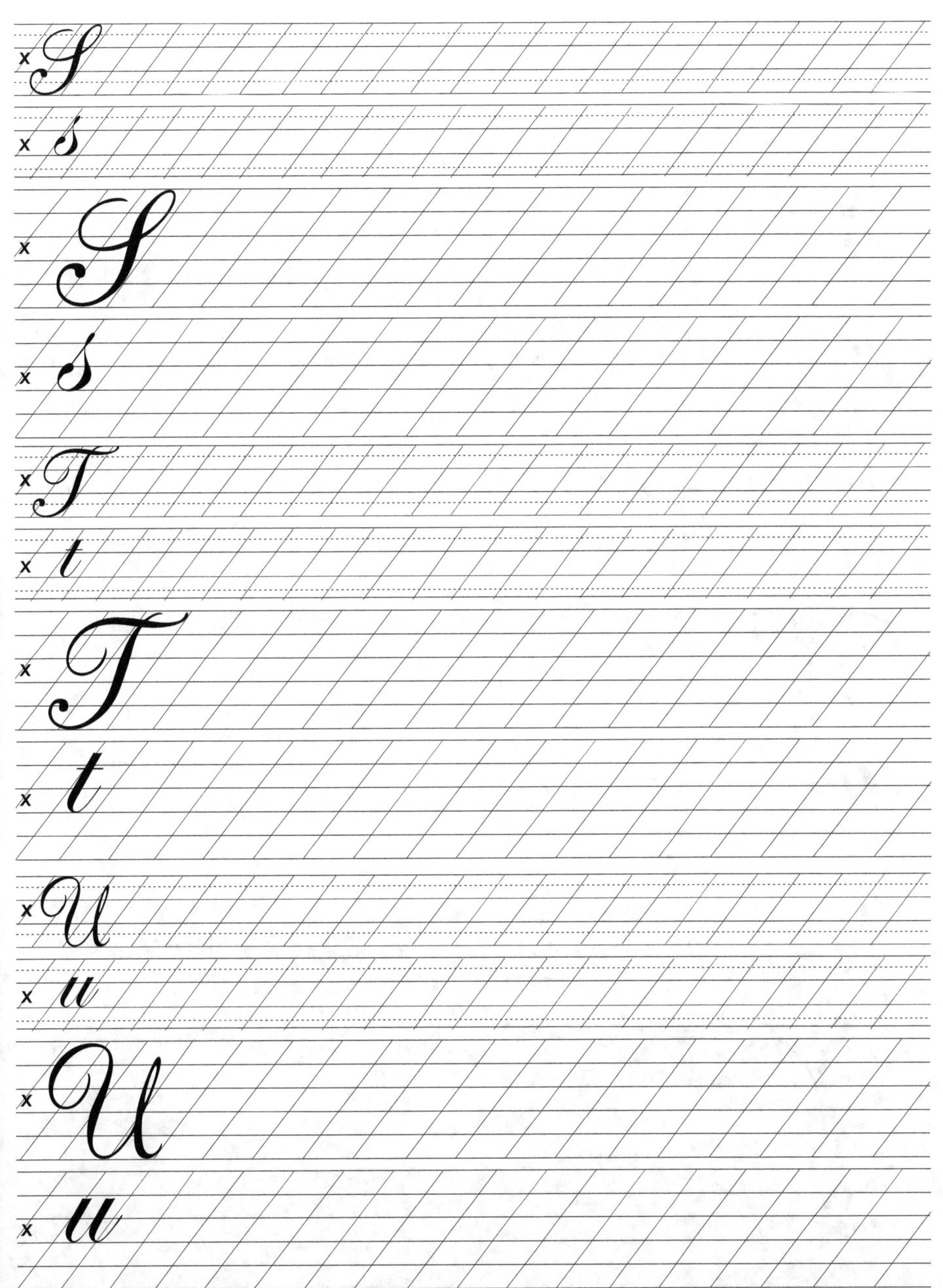

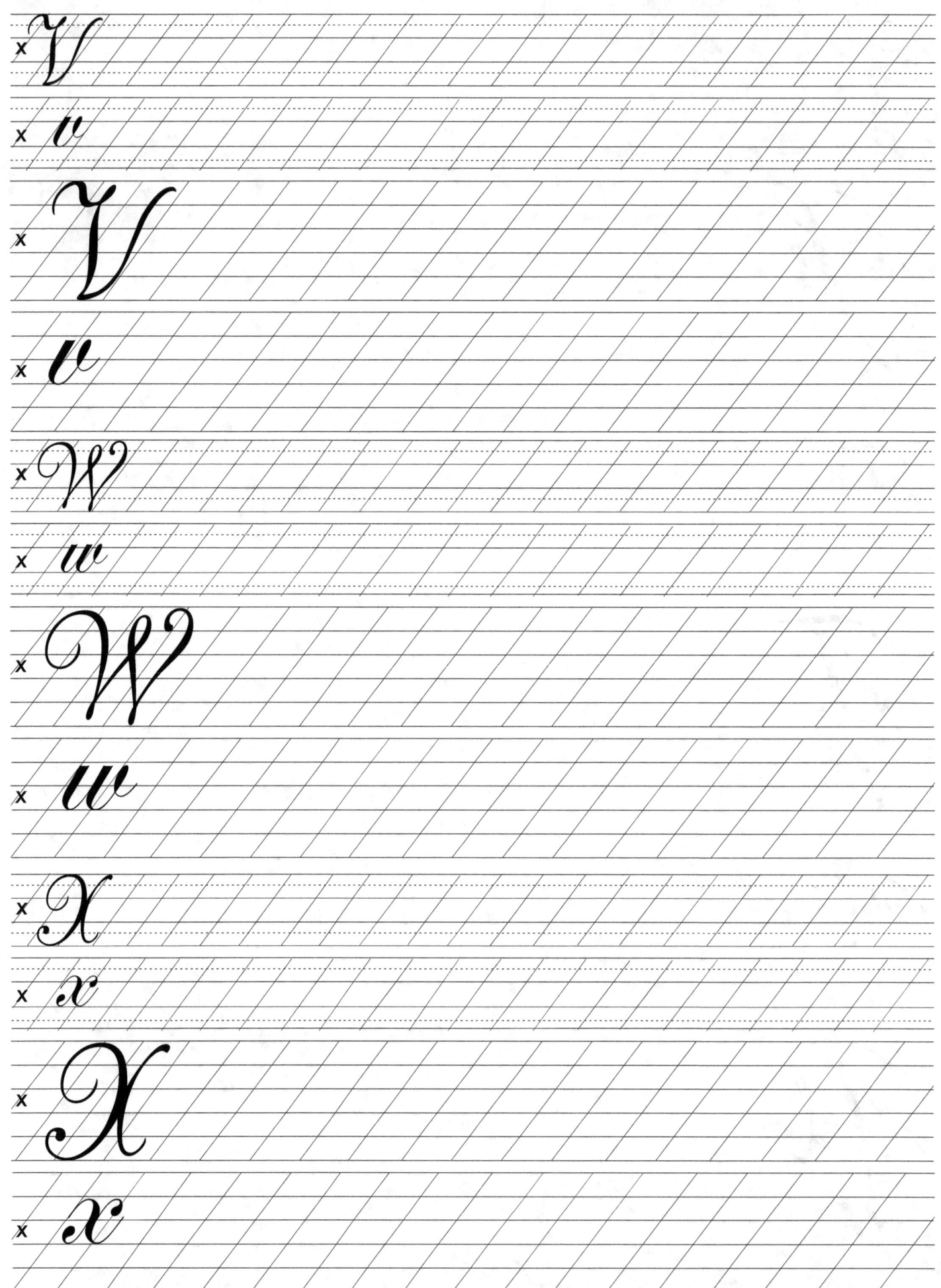

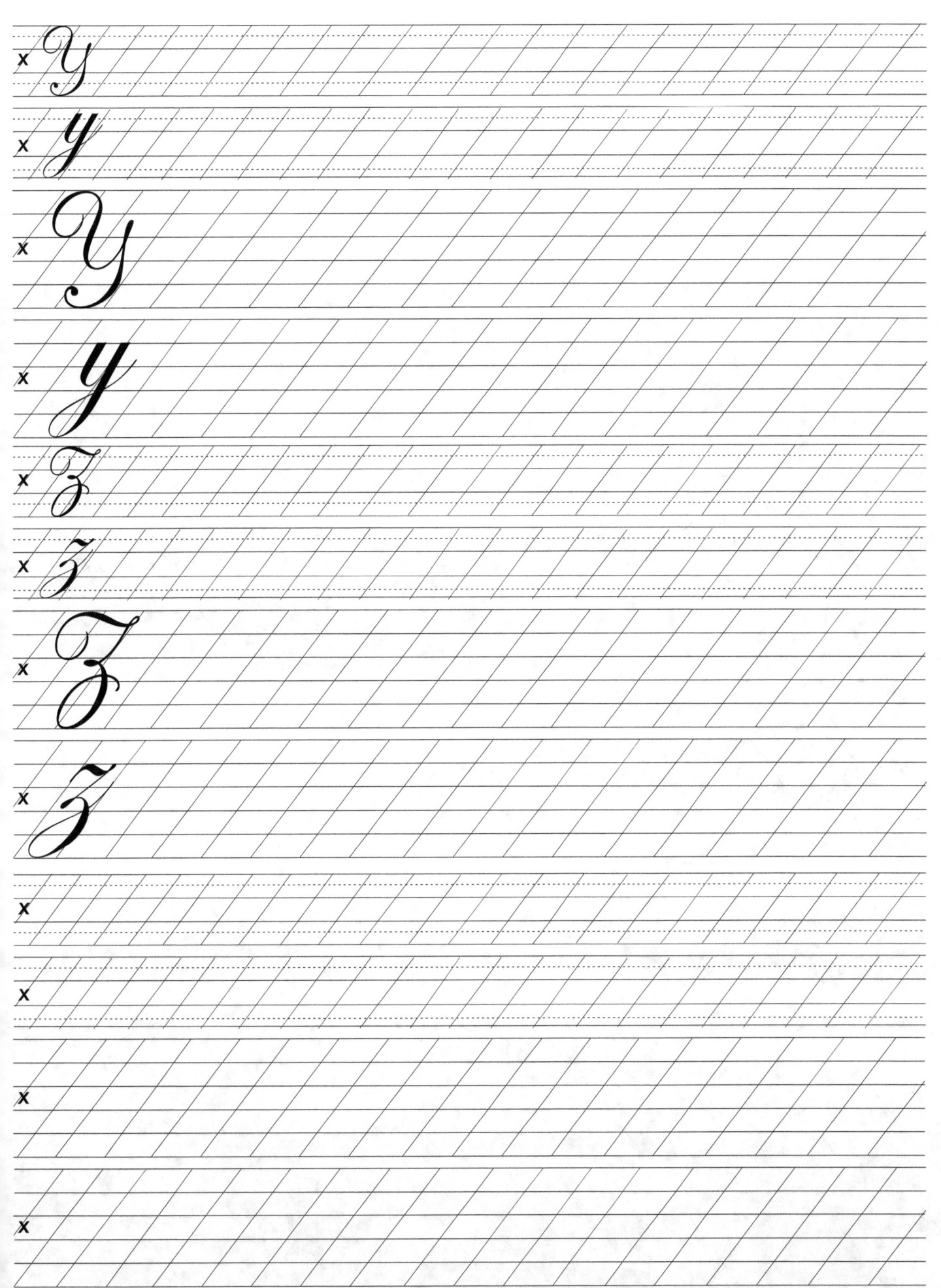

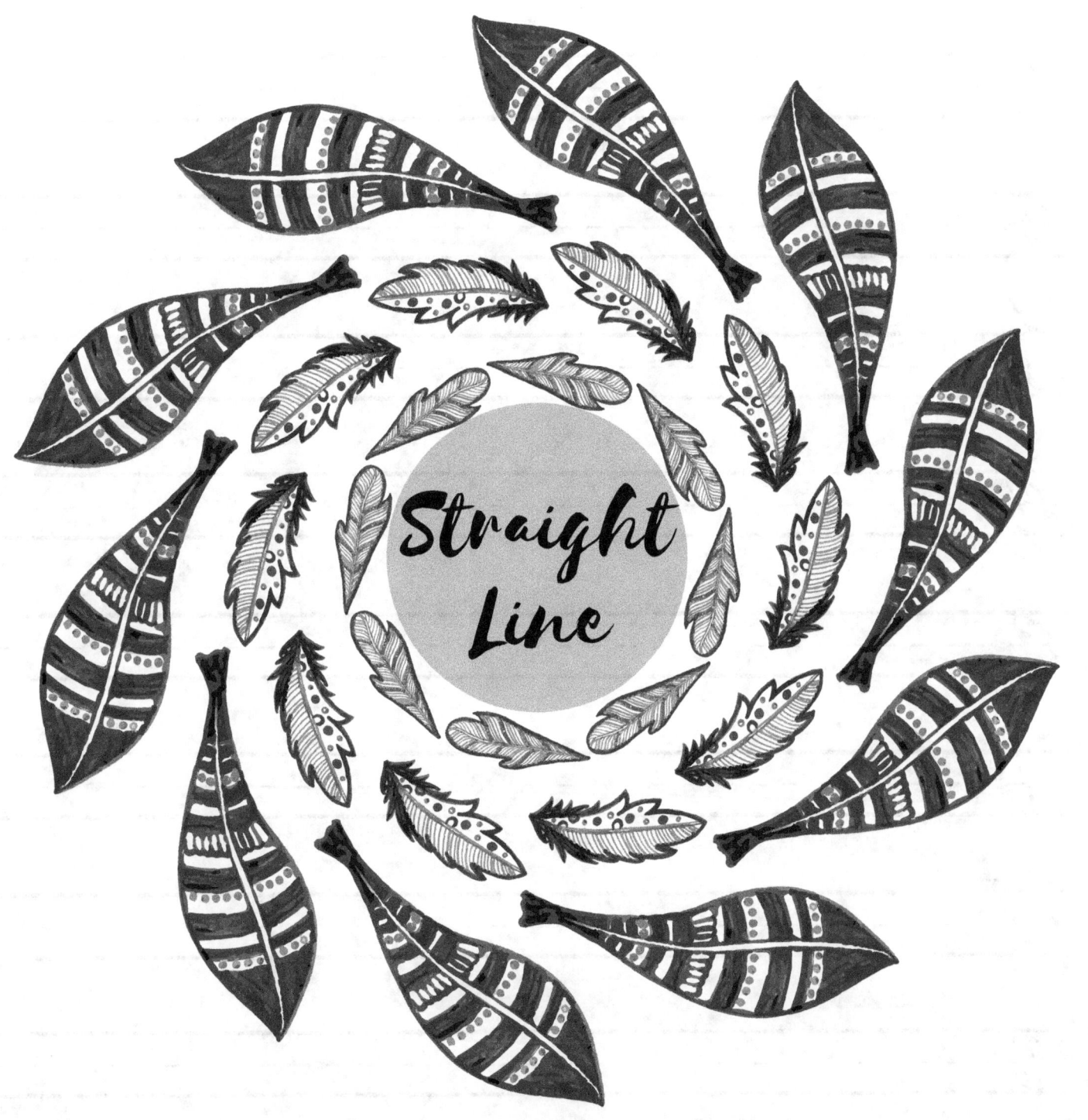

Straight Line

Part II

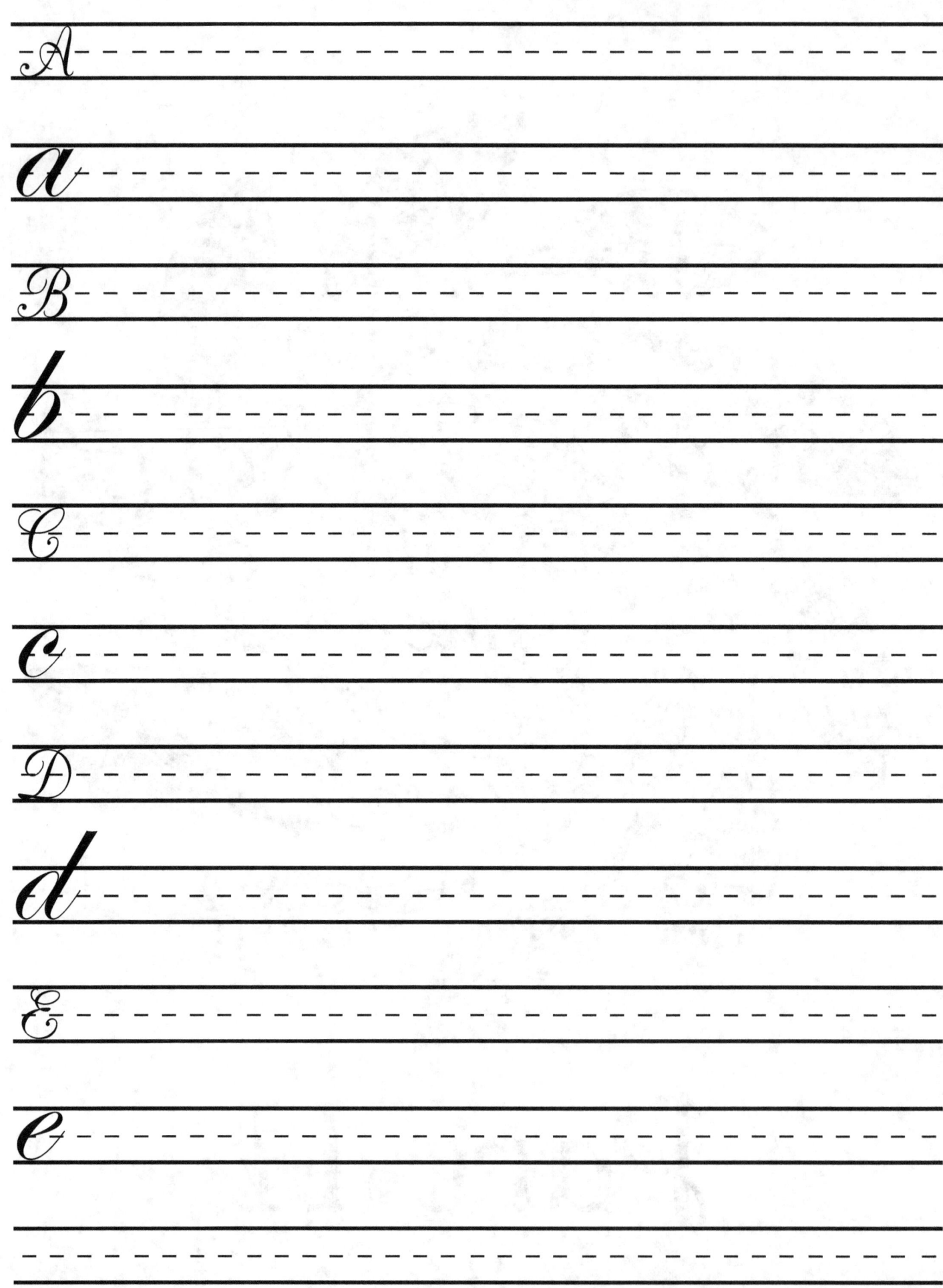

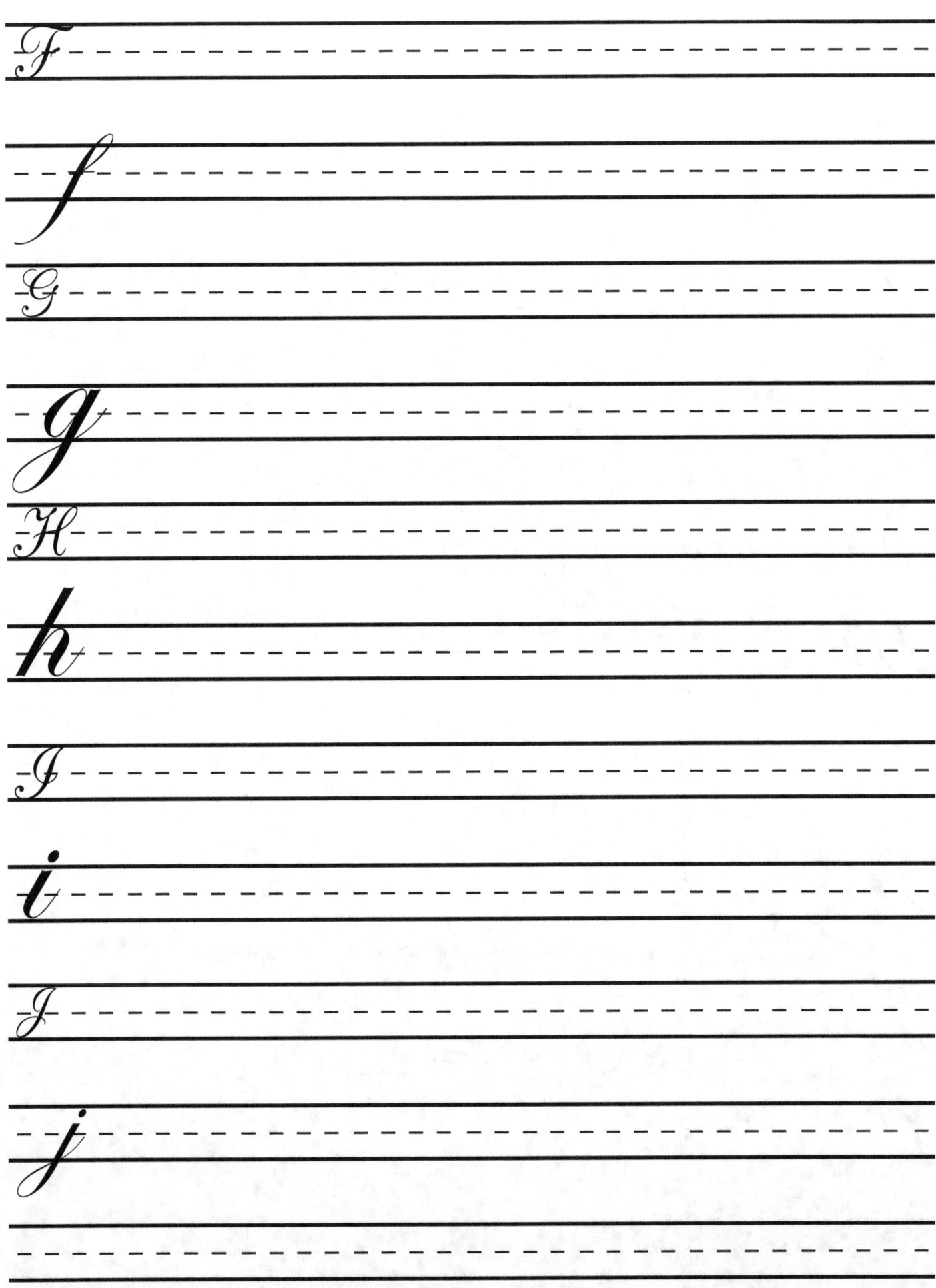

$\mathcal{K}$

$\boldsymbol{k}$

$\mathcal{L}$

$\boldsymbol{l}$

$\mathcal{M}$

$\boldsymbol{m}$

$\mathcal{N}$

$\boldsymbol{n}$

$\mathcal{O}$

$\boldsymbol{o}$

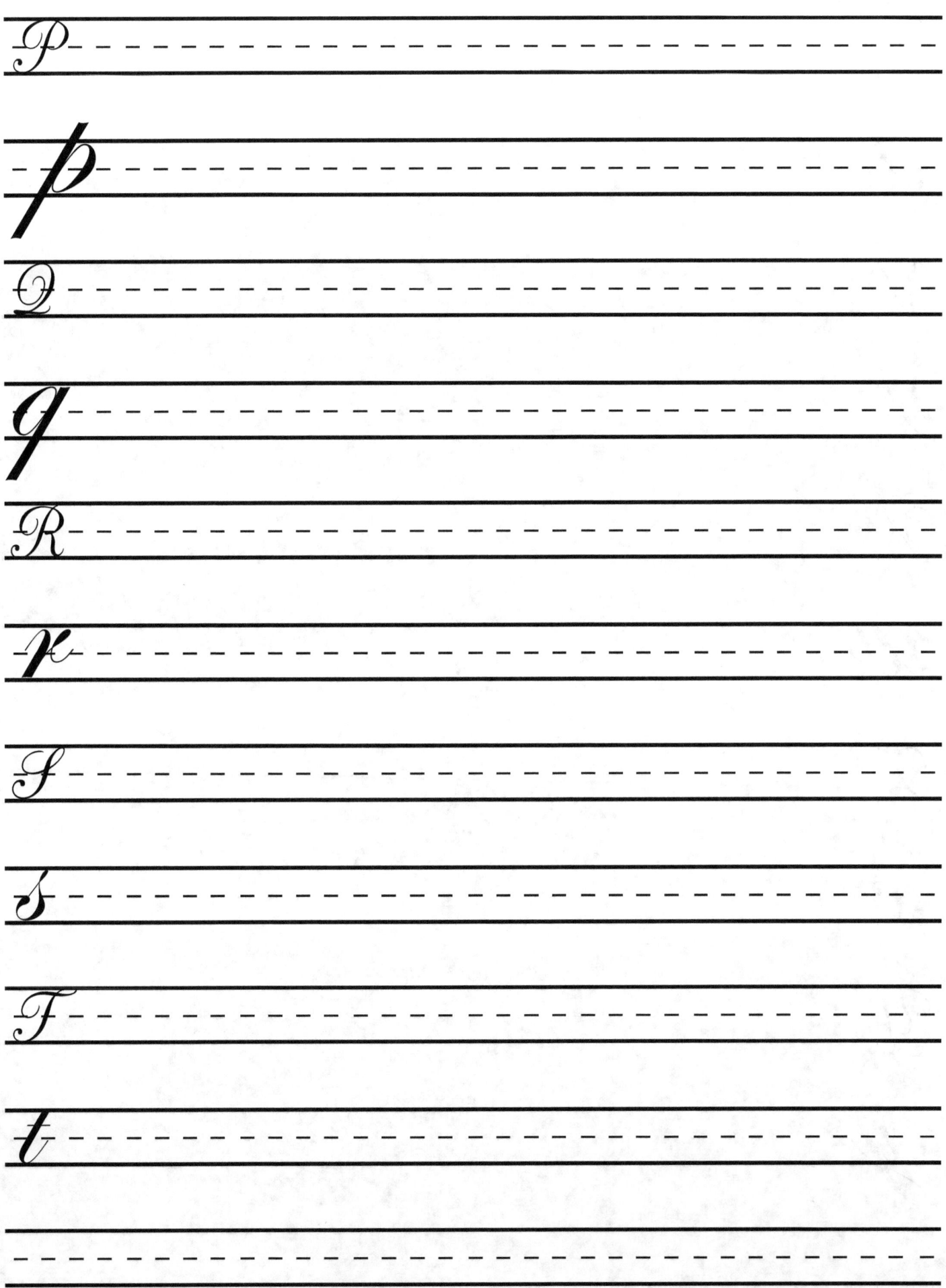

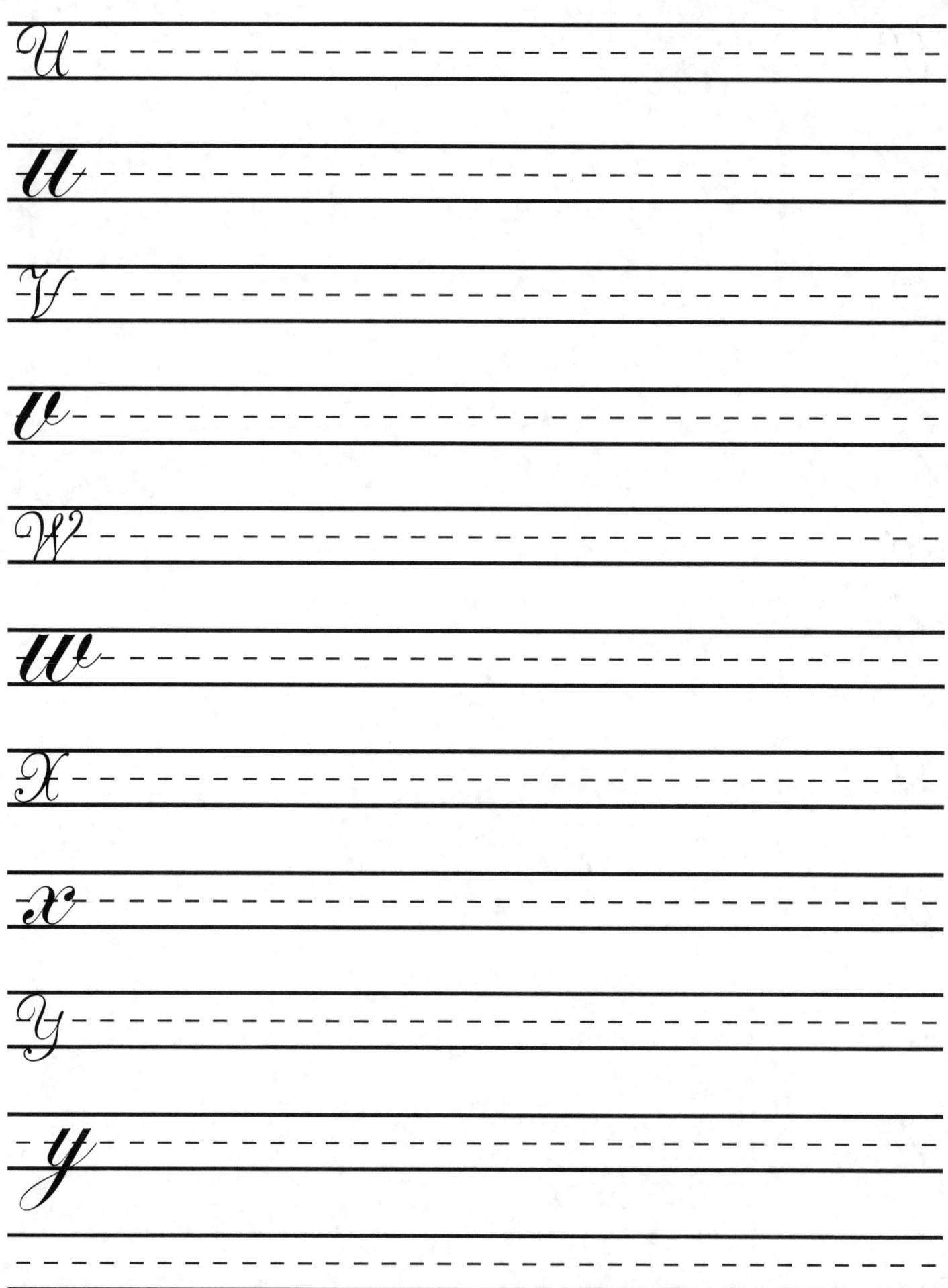

A

a

B

b

C

c

D

d

E

e

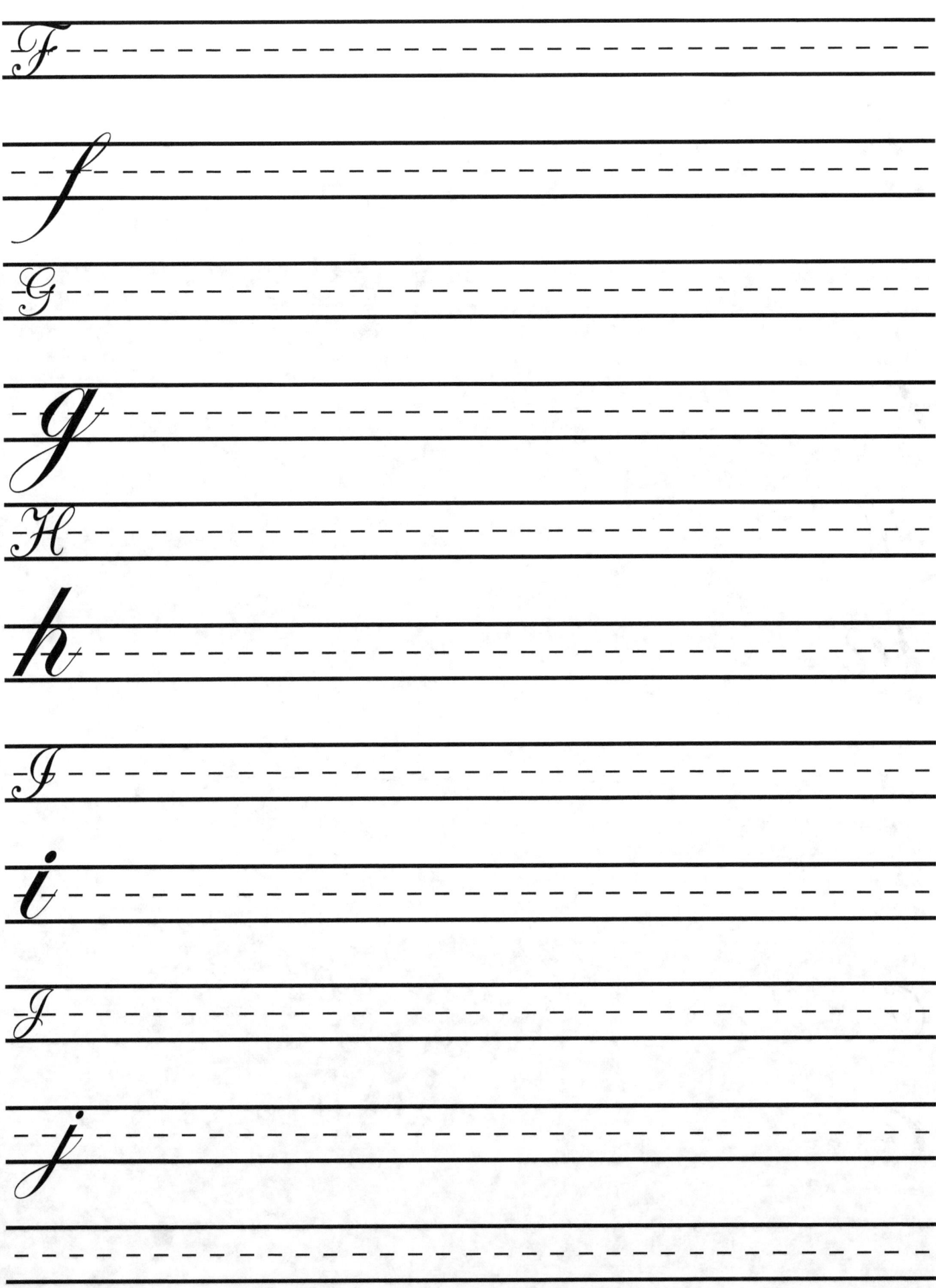

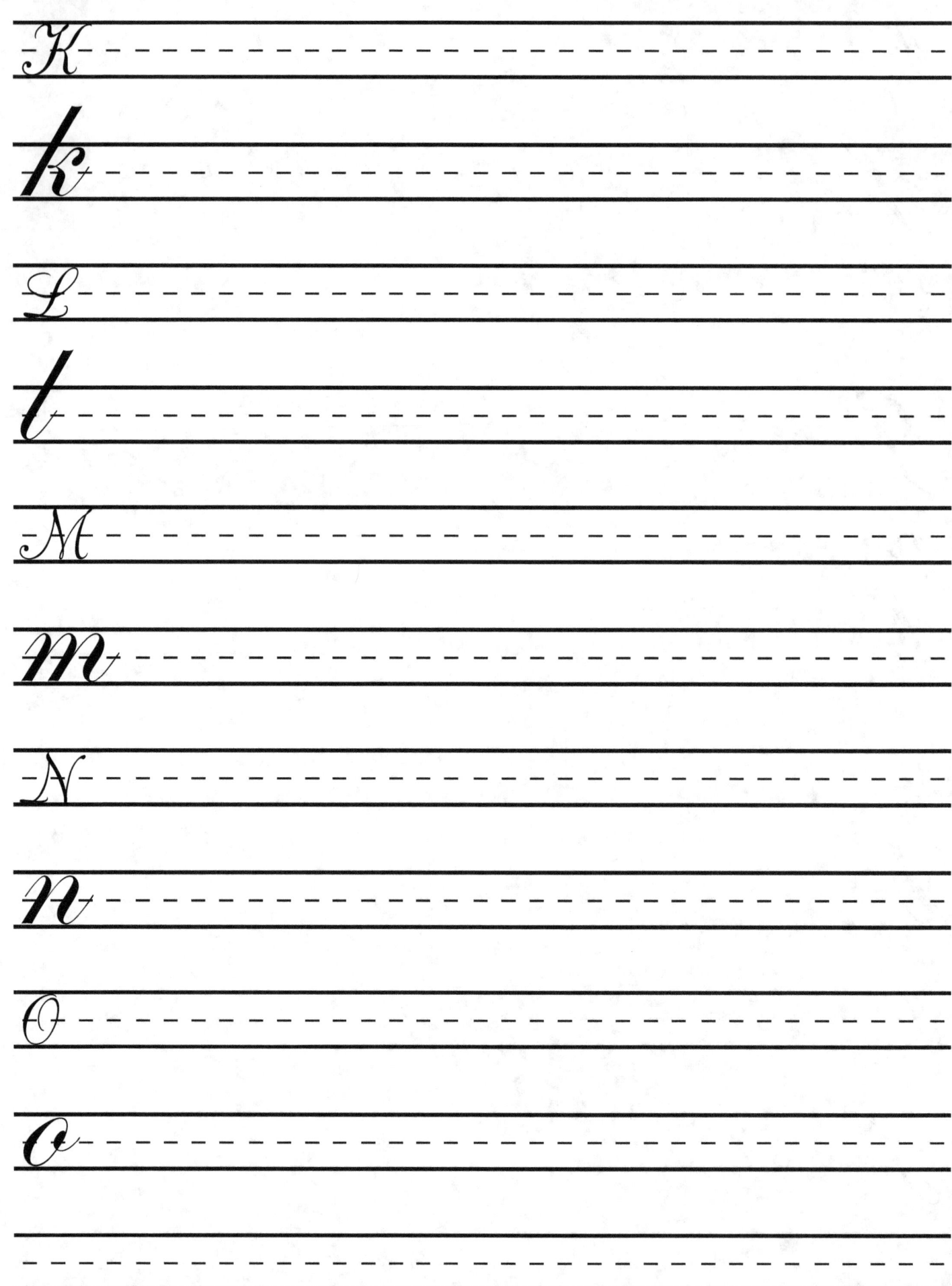

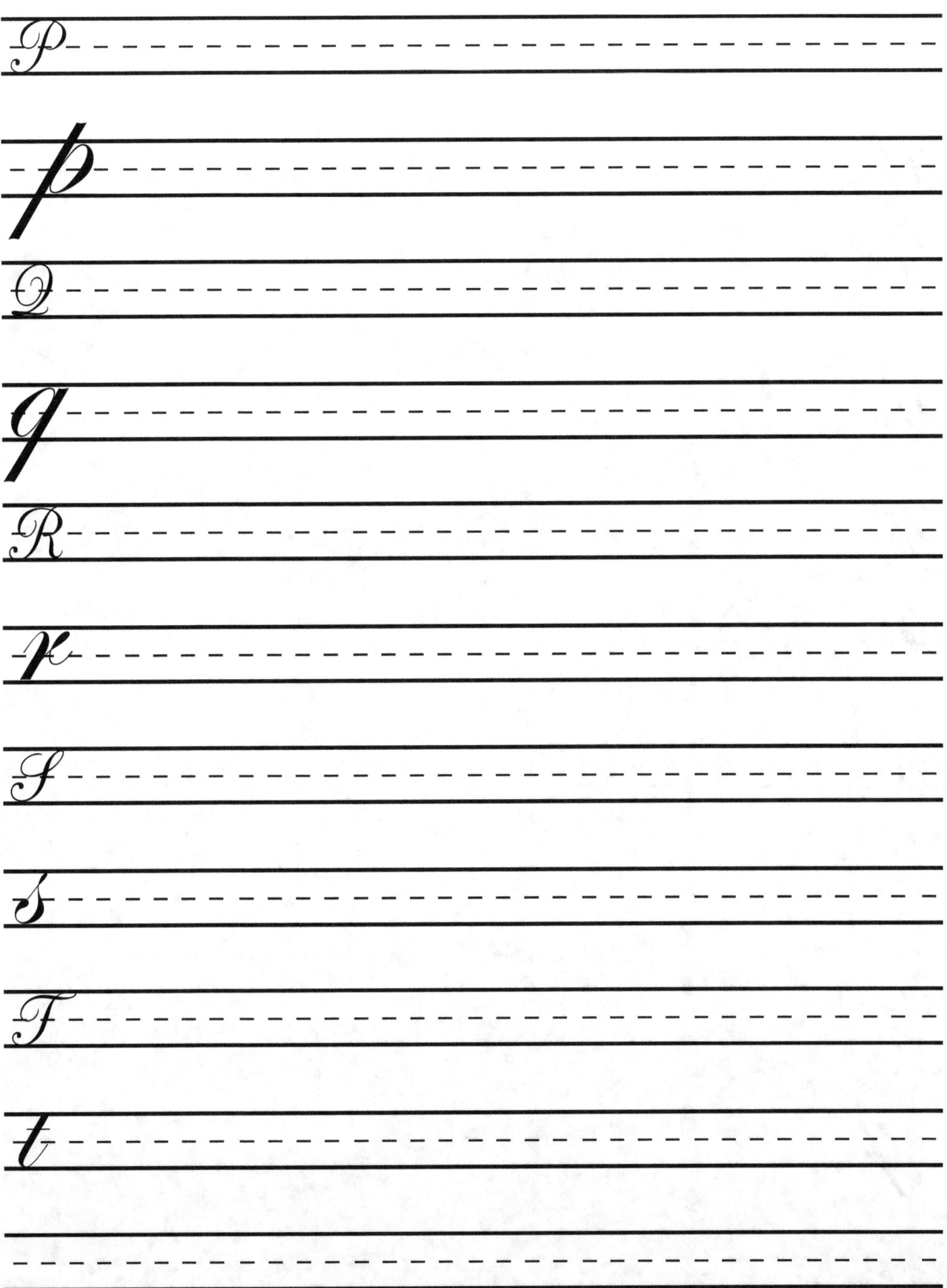

$\mathcal{U}$ ---

u ---

$\mathcal{V}$ ---

v ---

$\mathcal{W}$ ---

w ---

$\mathcal{X}$ ---

x ---

$\mathcal{Y}$ ---

y ---

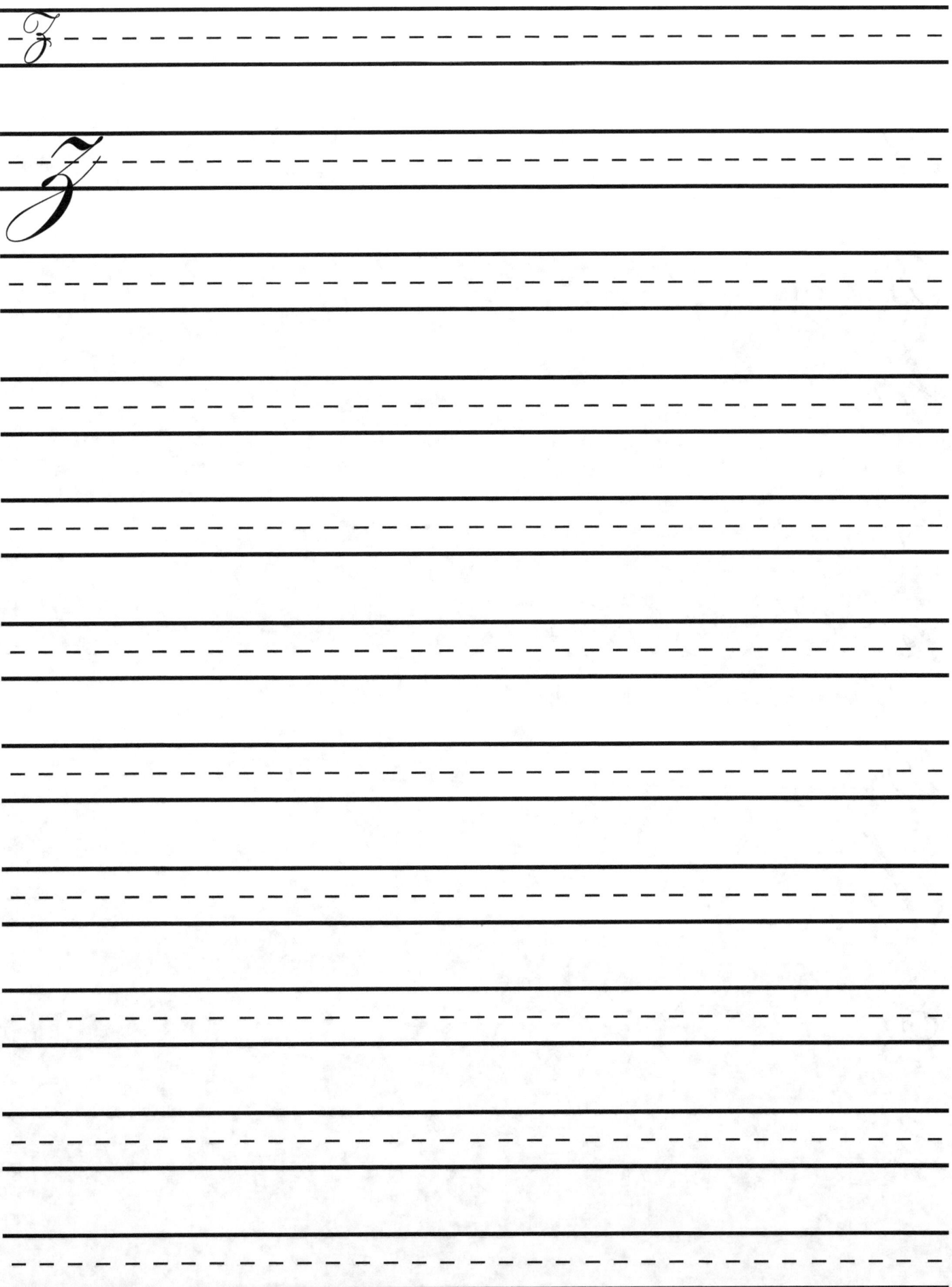

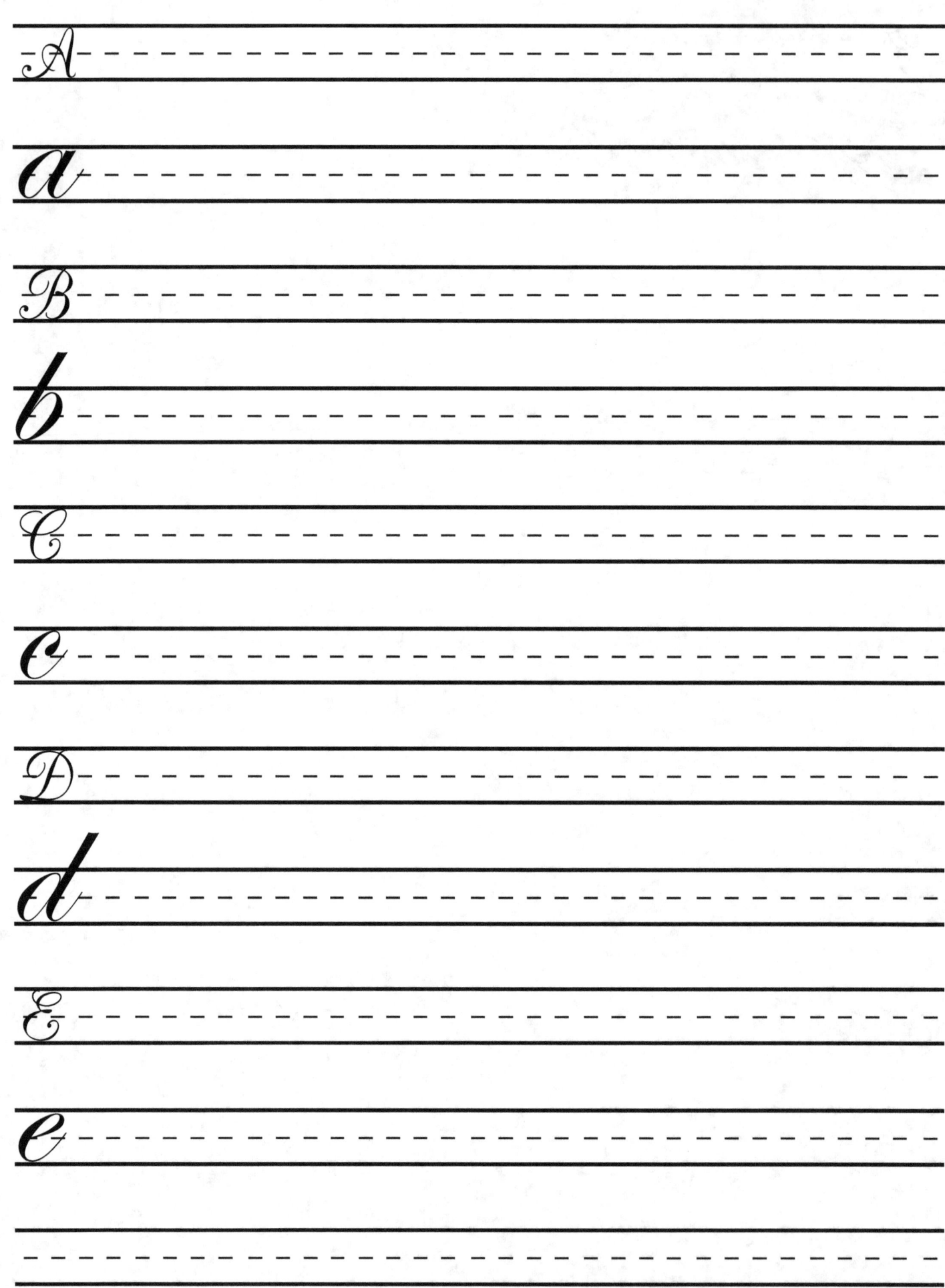

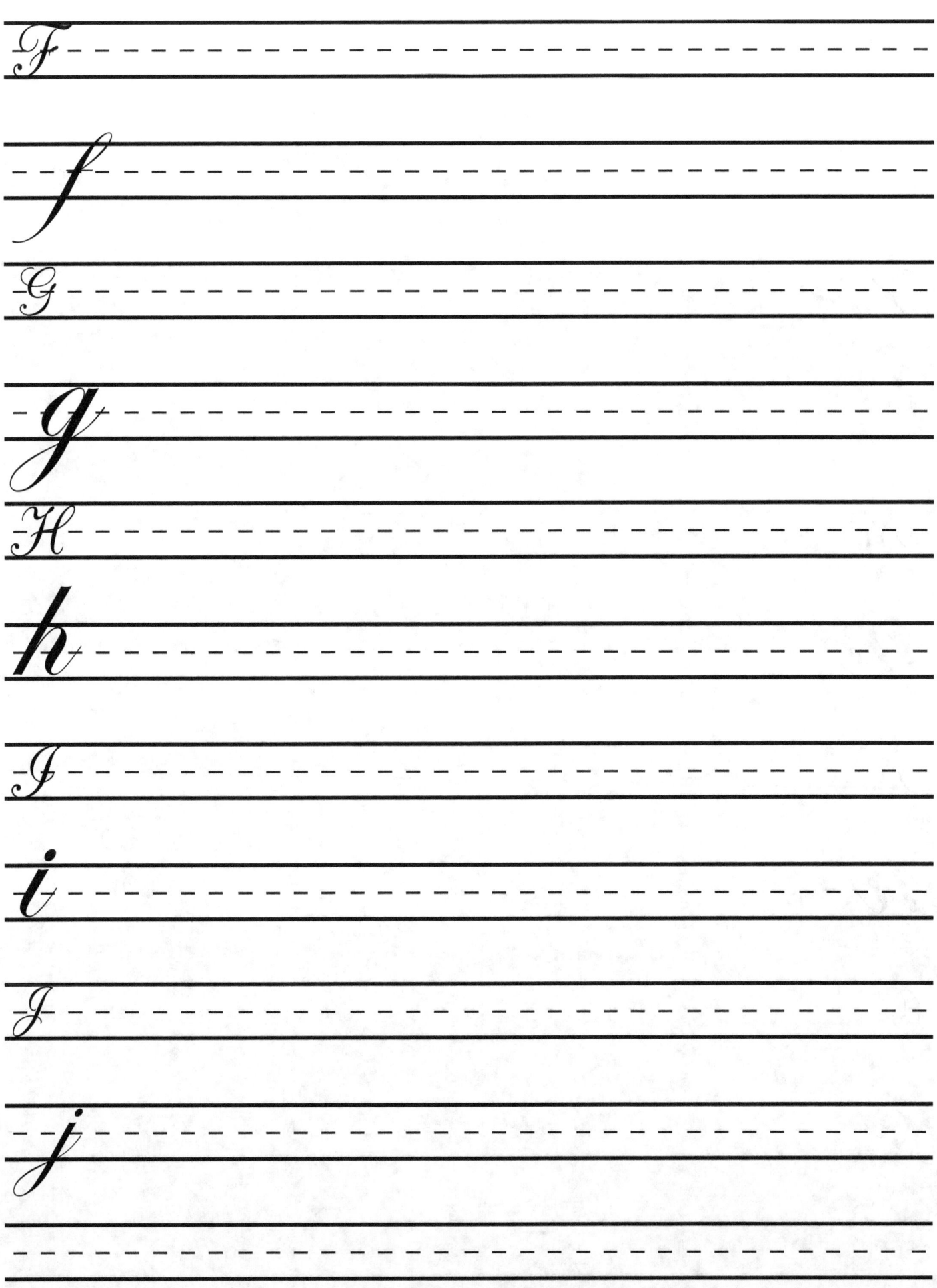

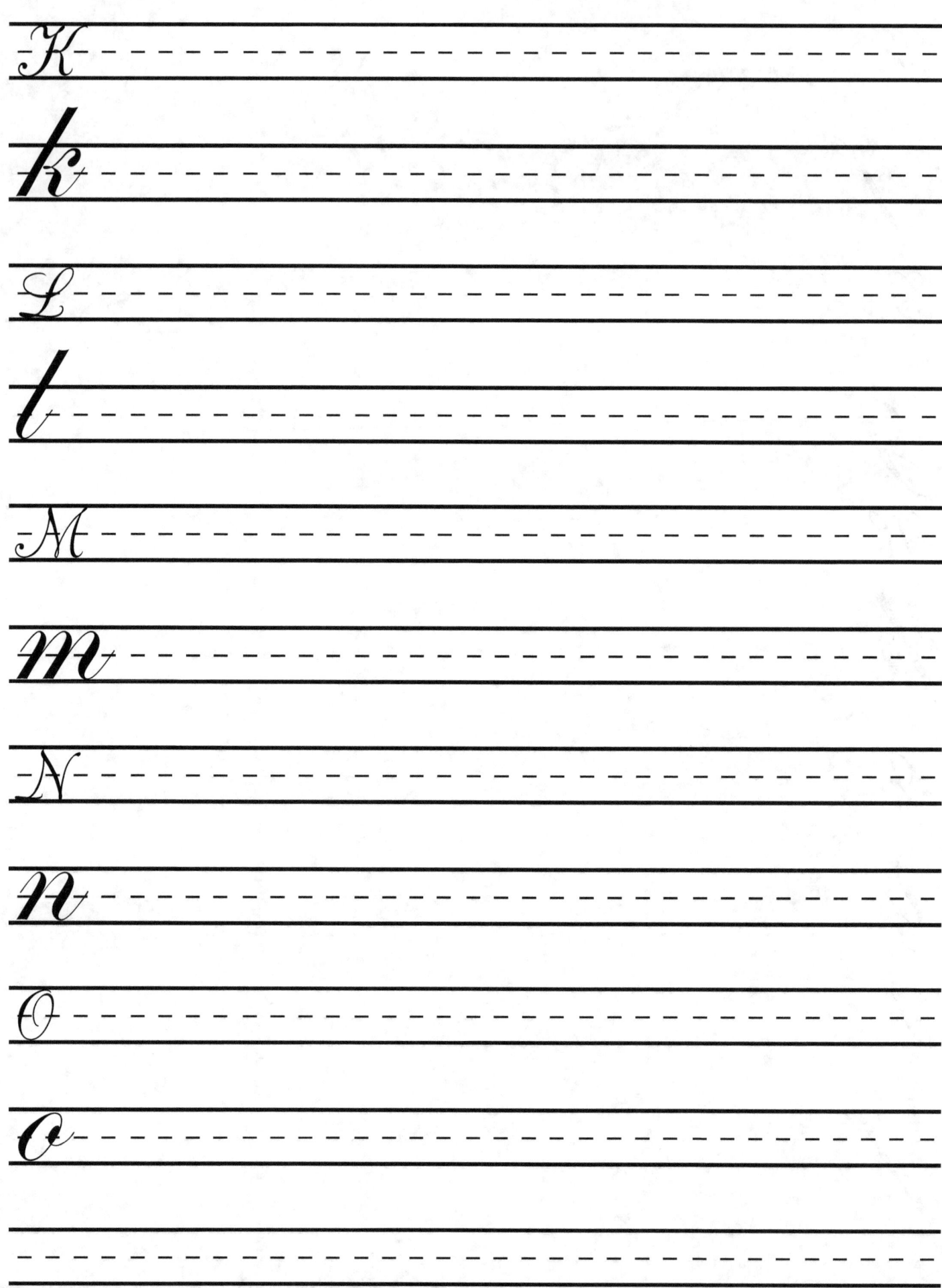

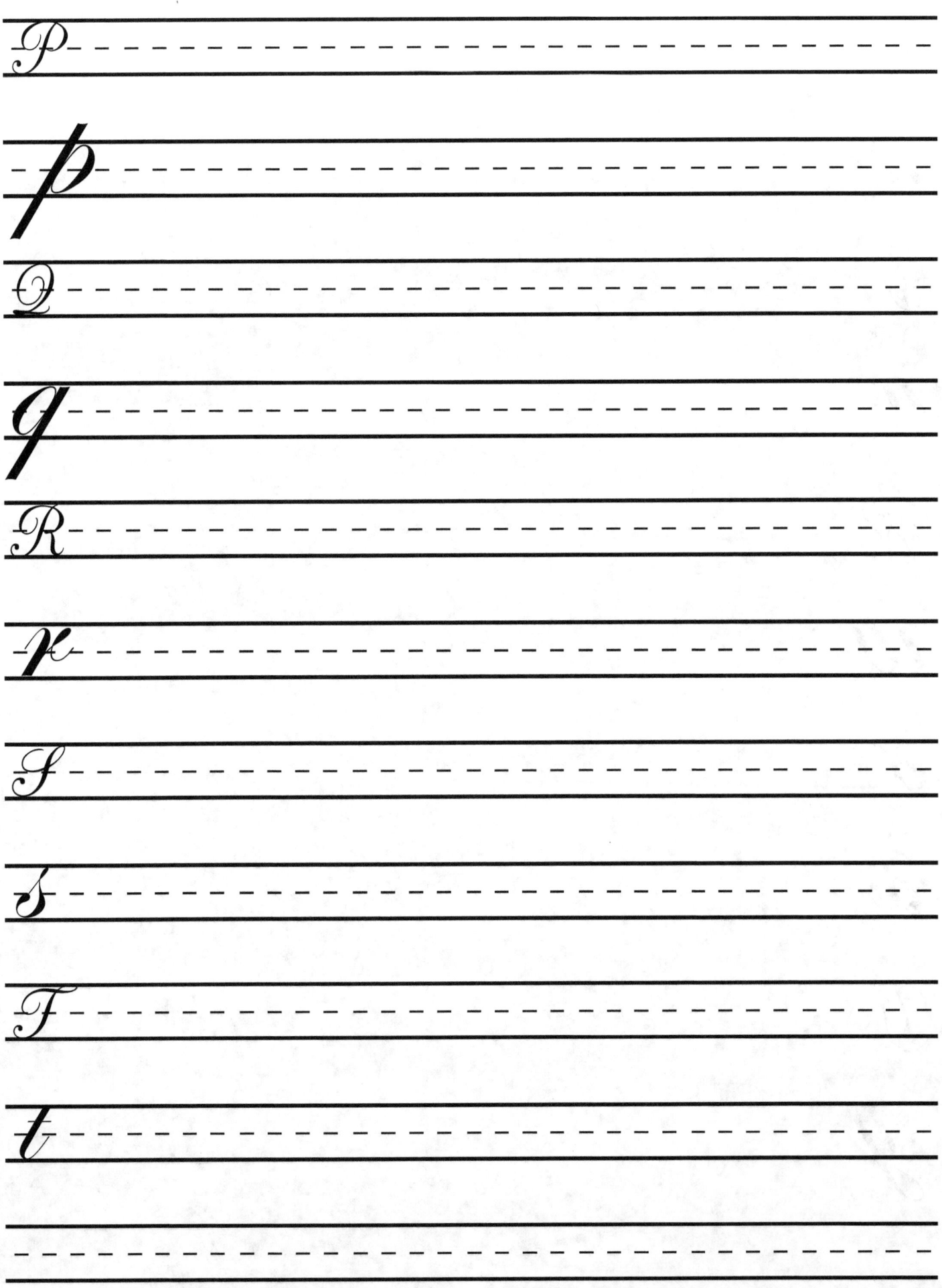

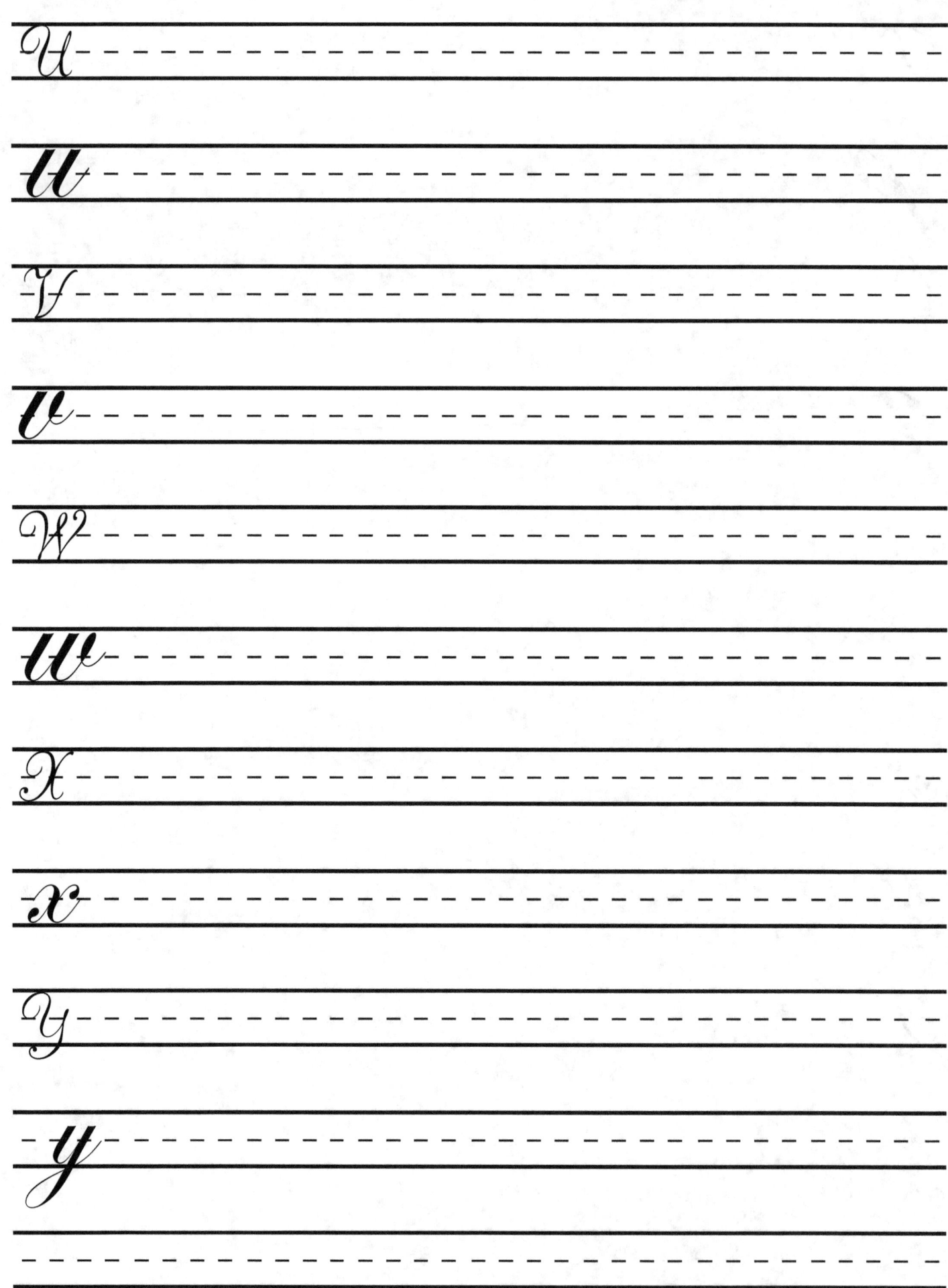

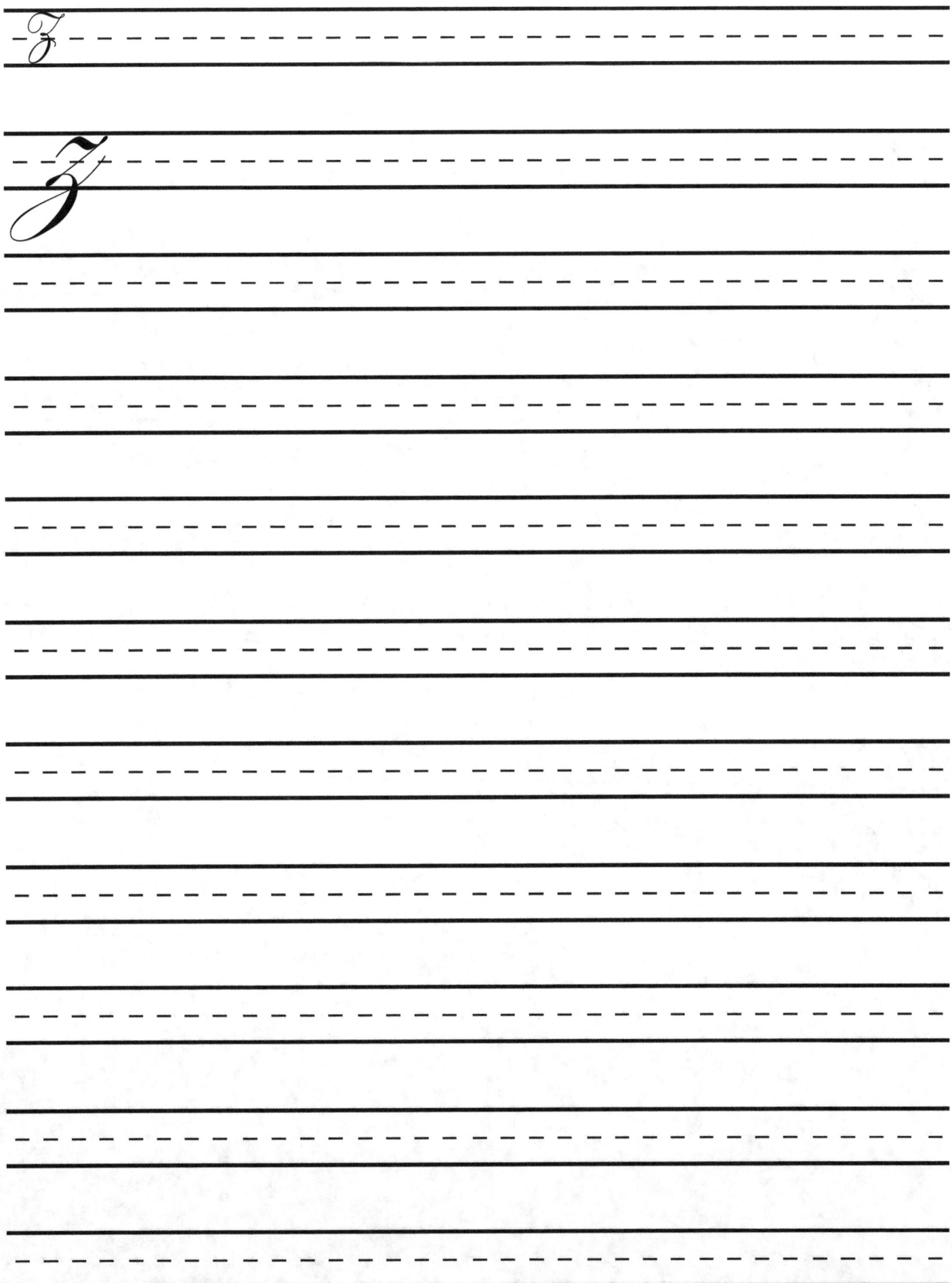

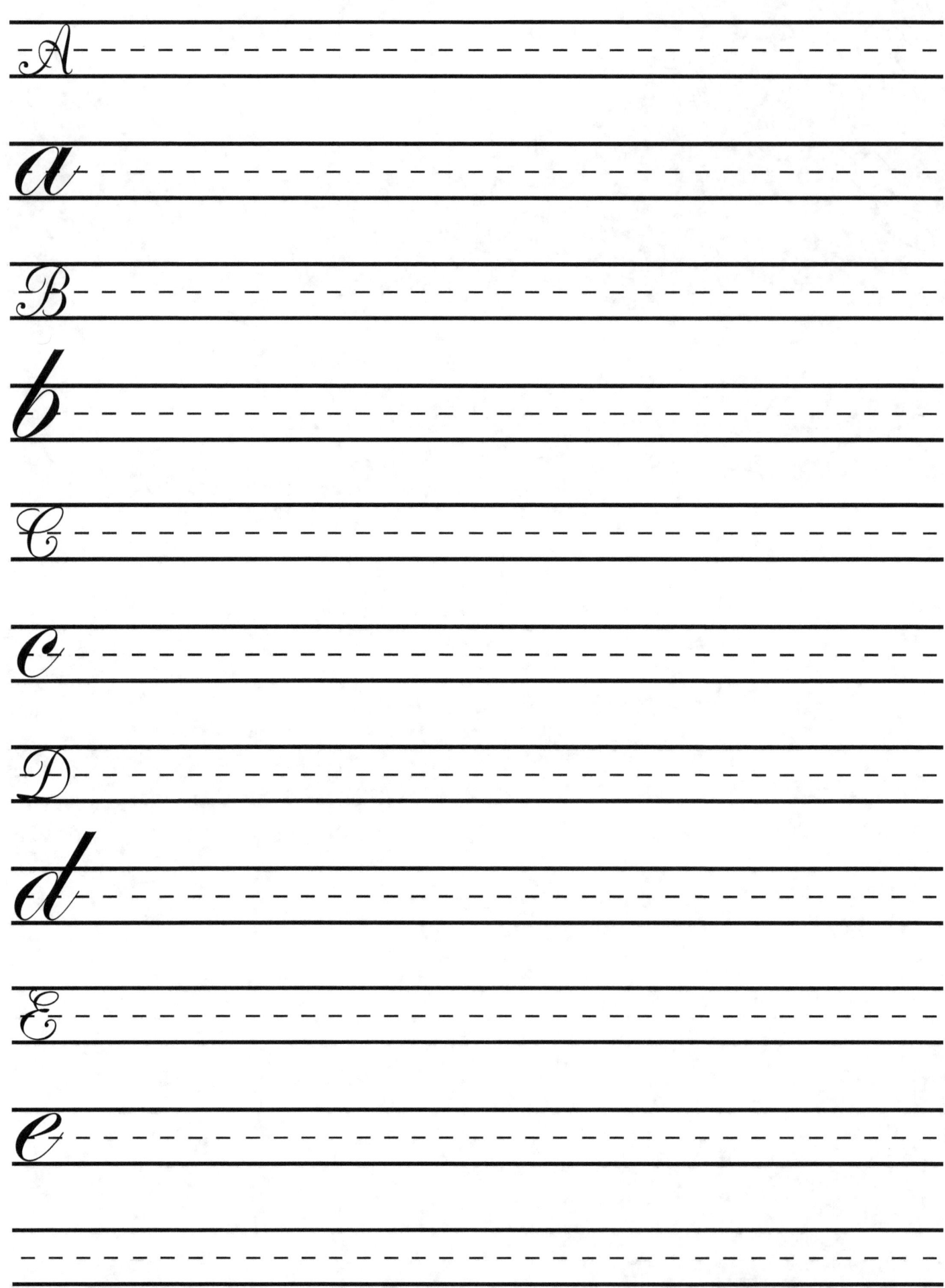

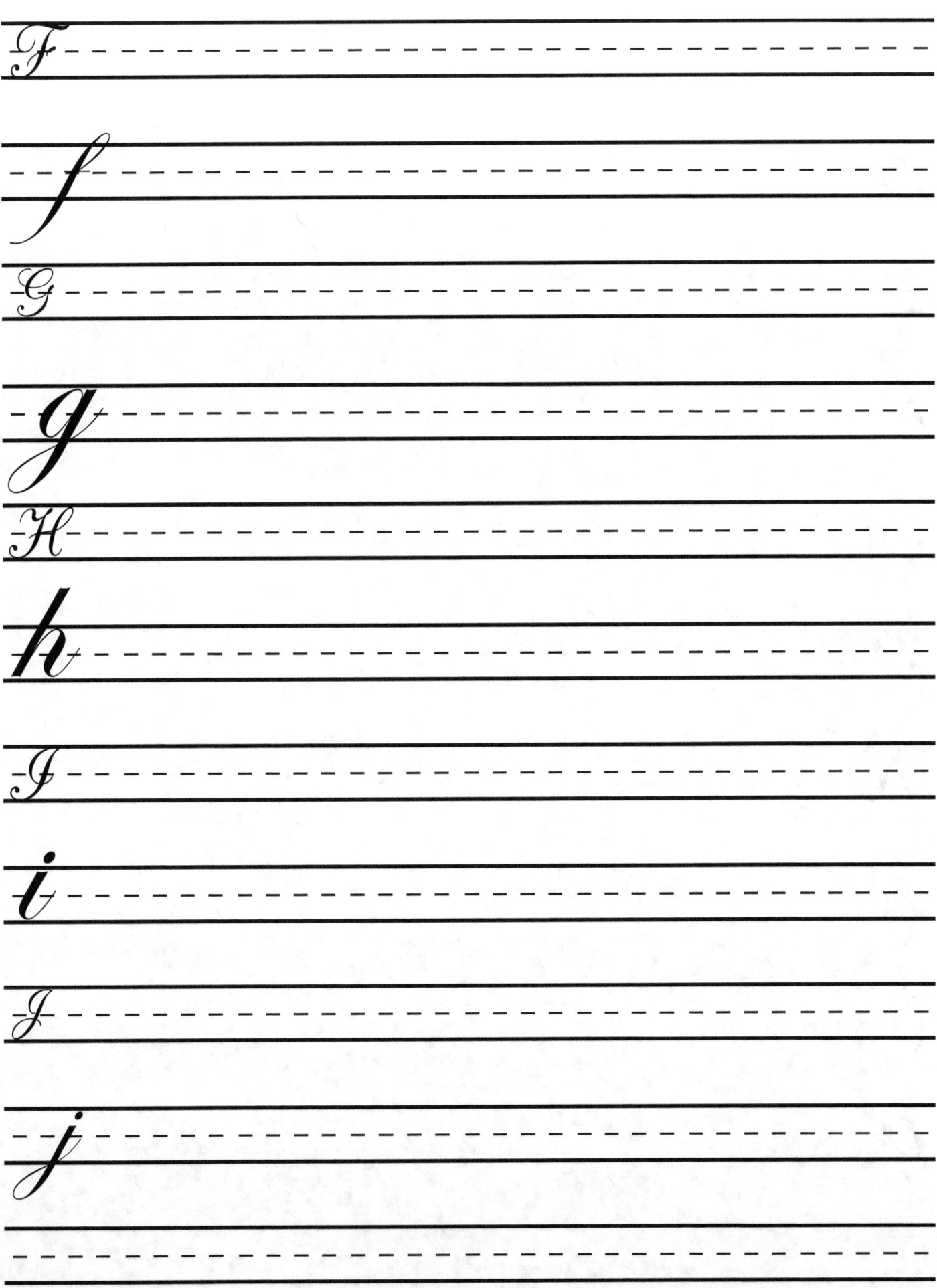

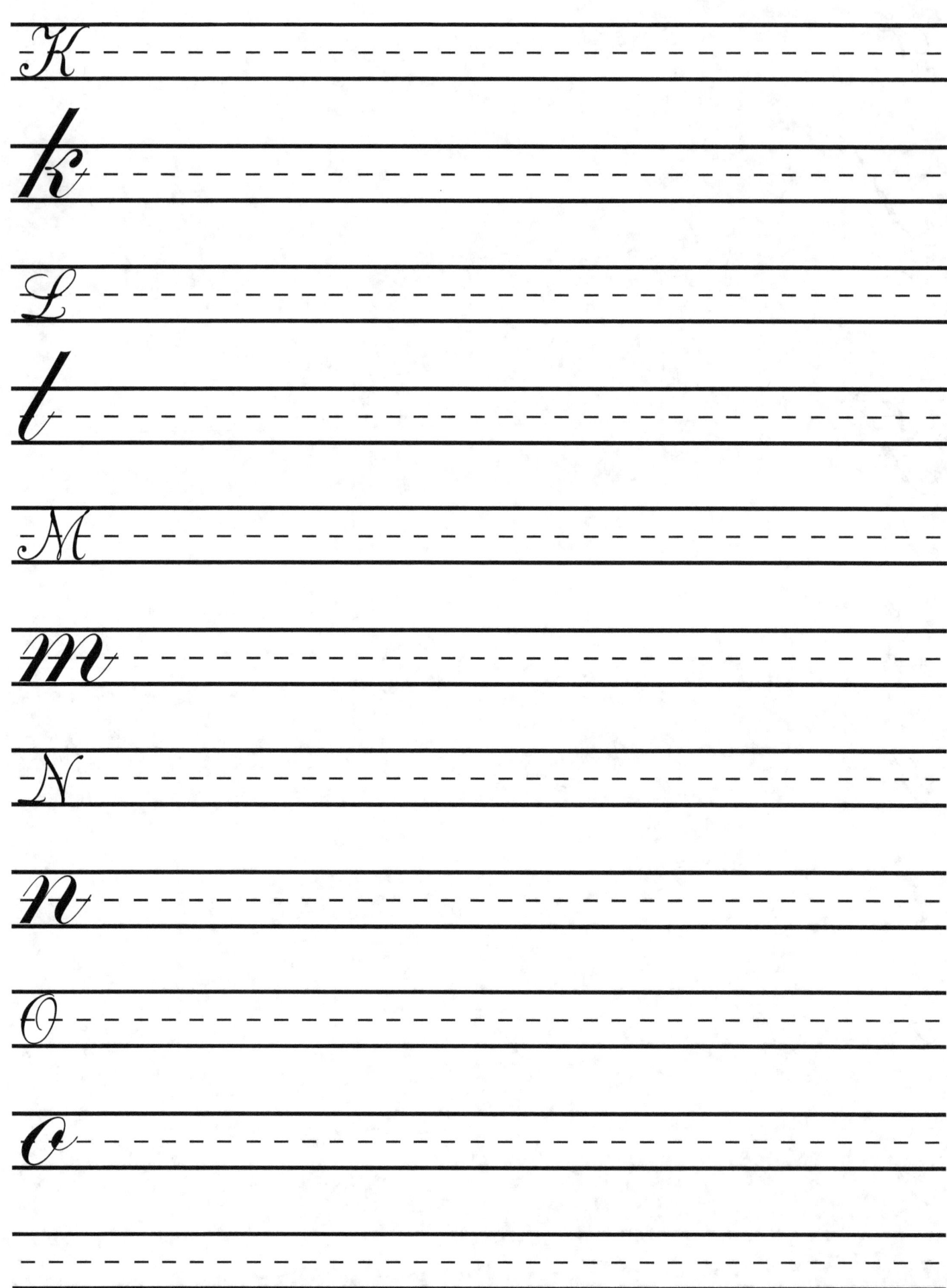

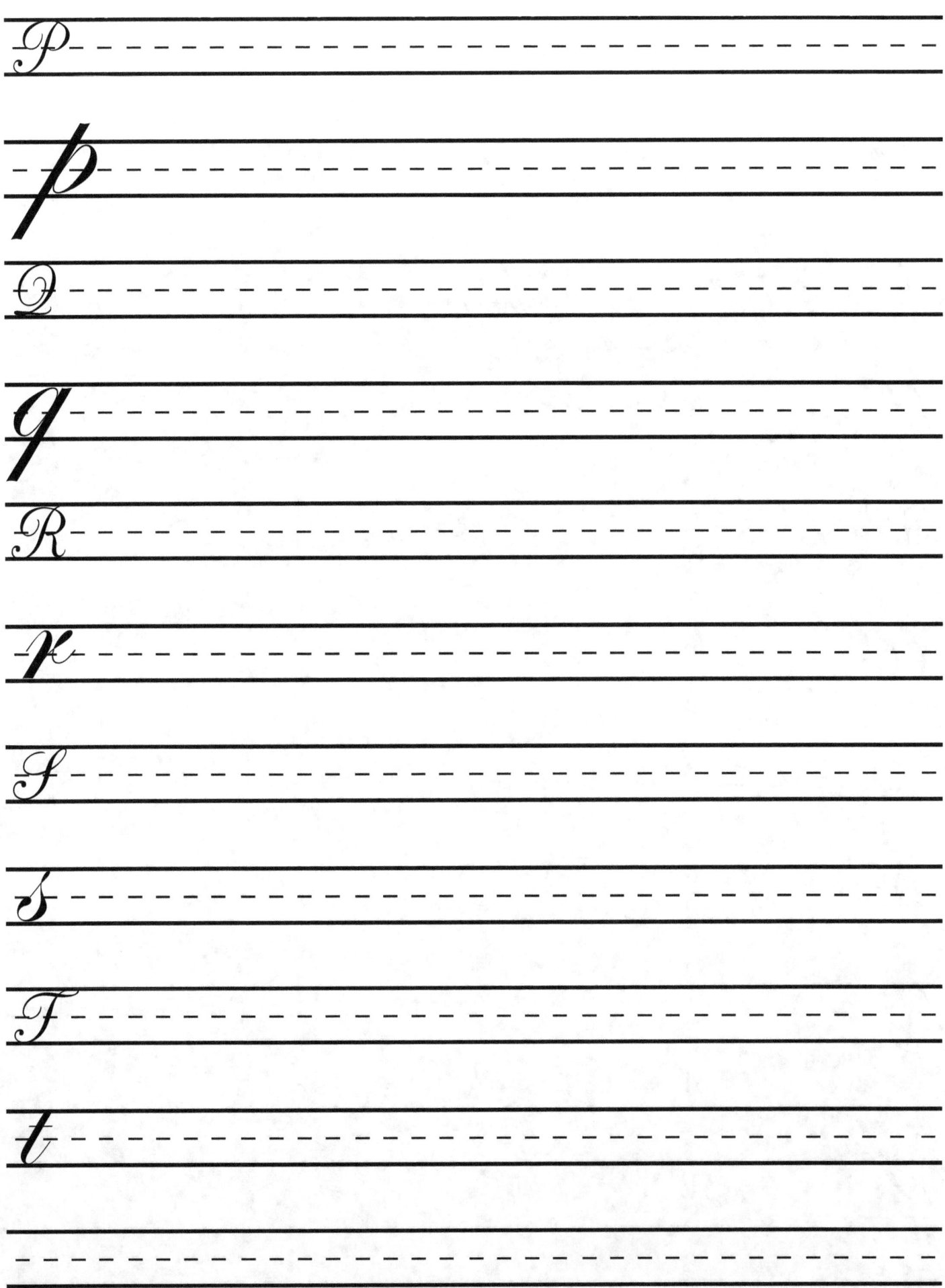

$\mathcal{U}$

$\boldsymbol{u}$

$\mathcal{V}$

$\boldsymbol{v}$

$\mathcal{W}$

$\boldsymbol{w}$

$\mathcal{X}$

$\boldsymbol{x}$

$\mathcal{Y}$

$\boldsymbol{y}$

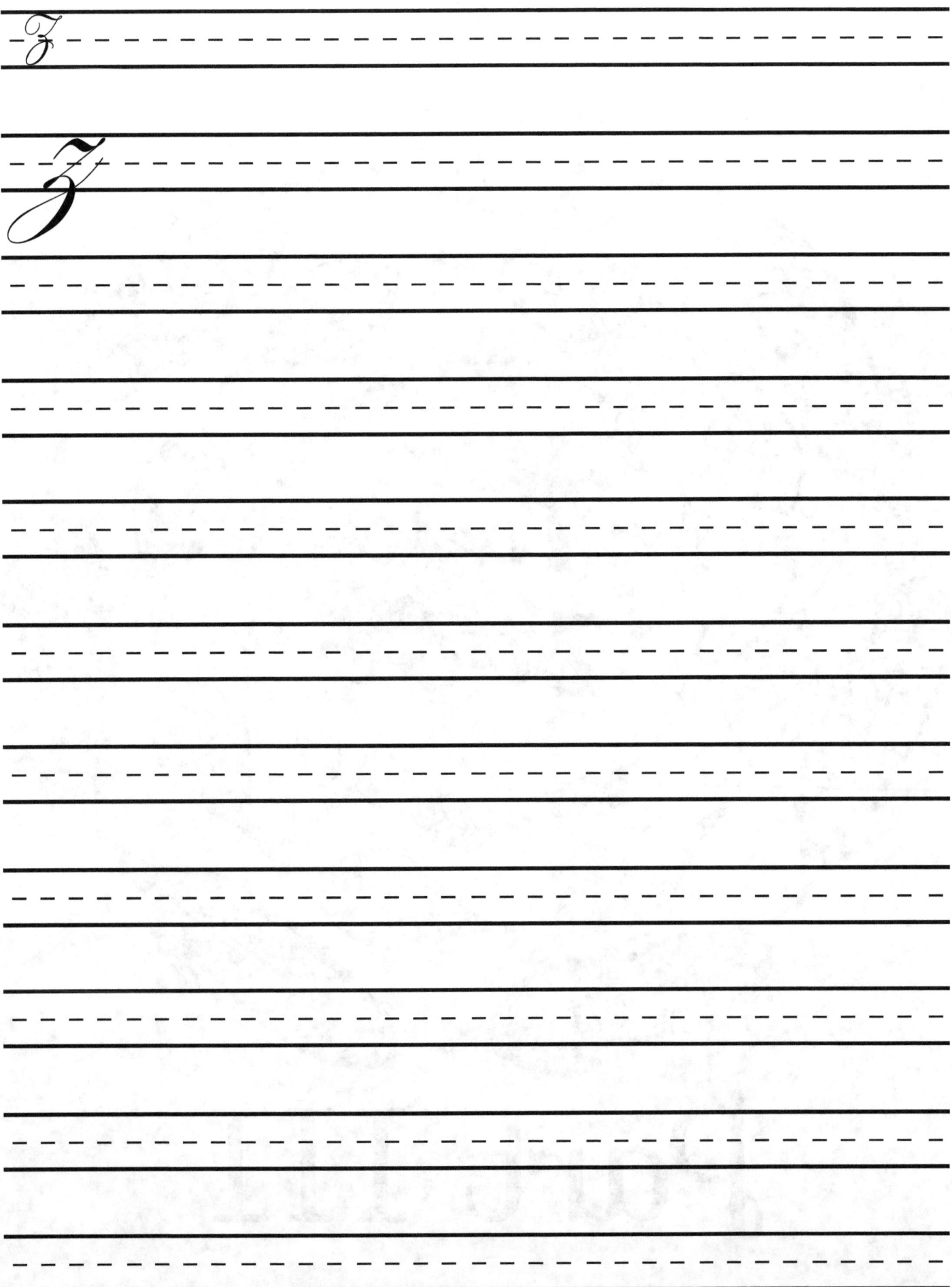

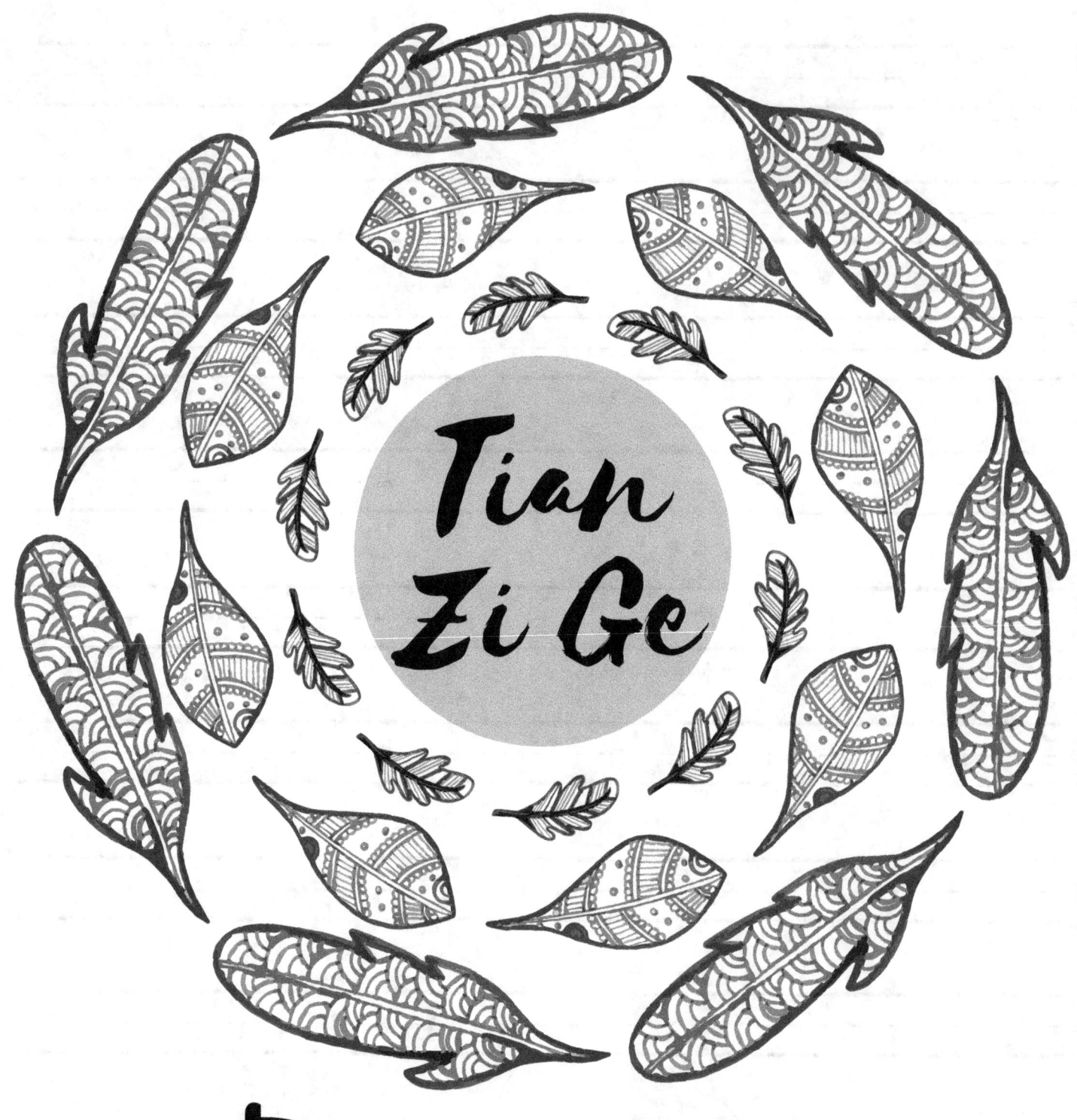

Tian Zi Ge

Part III

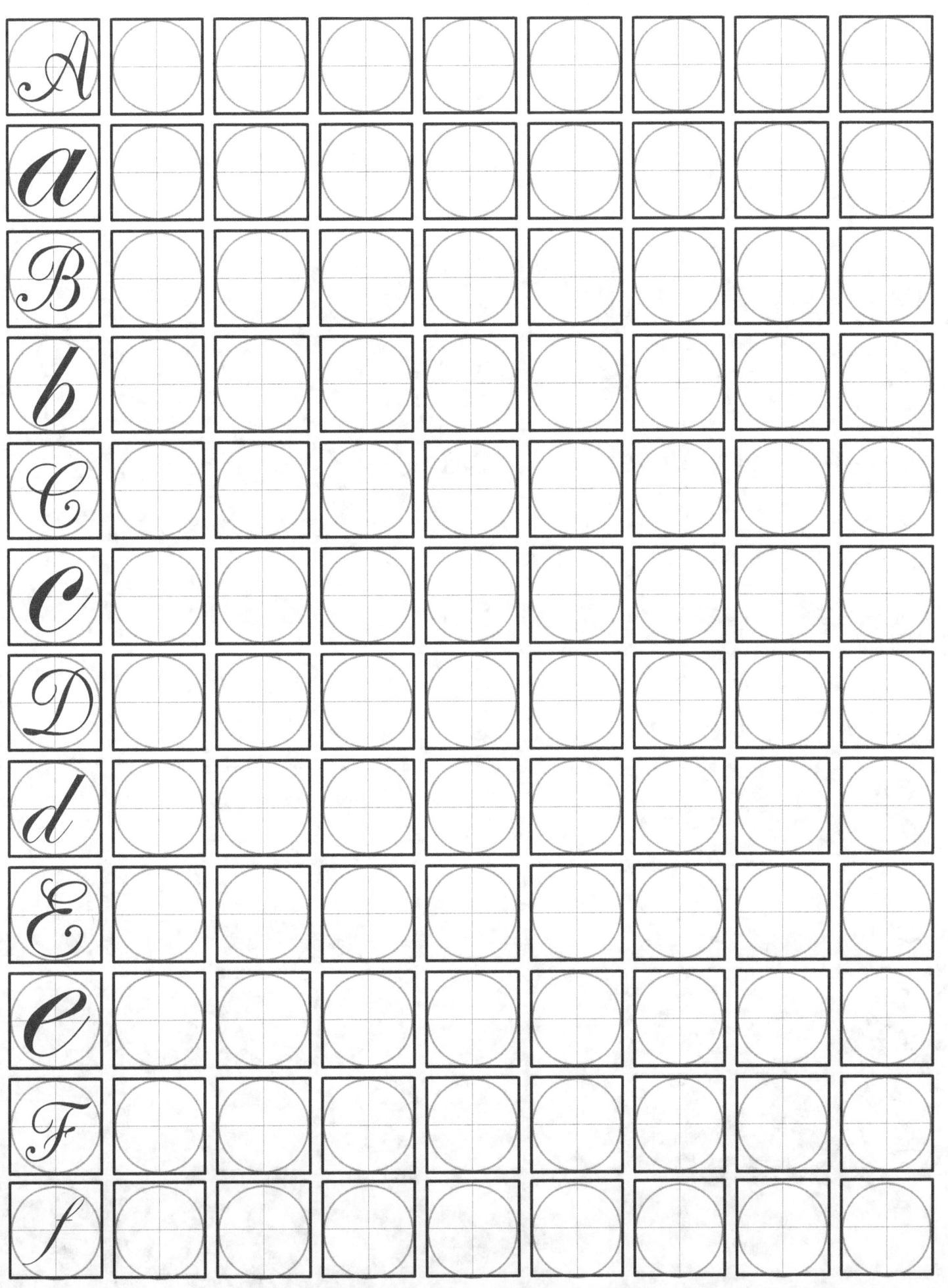

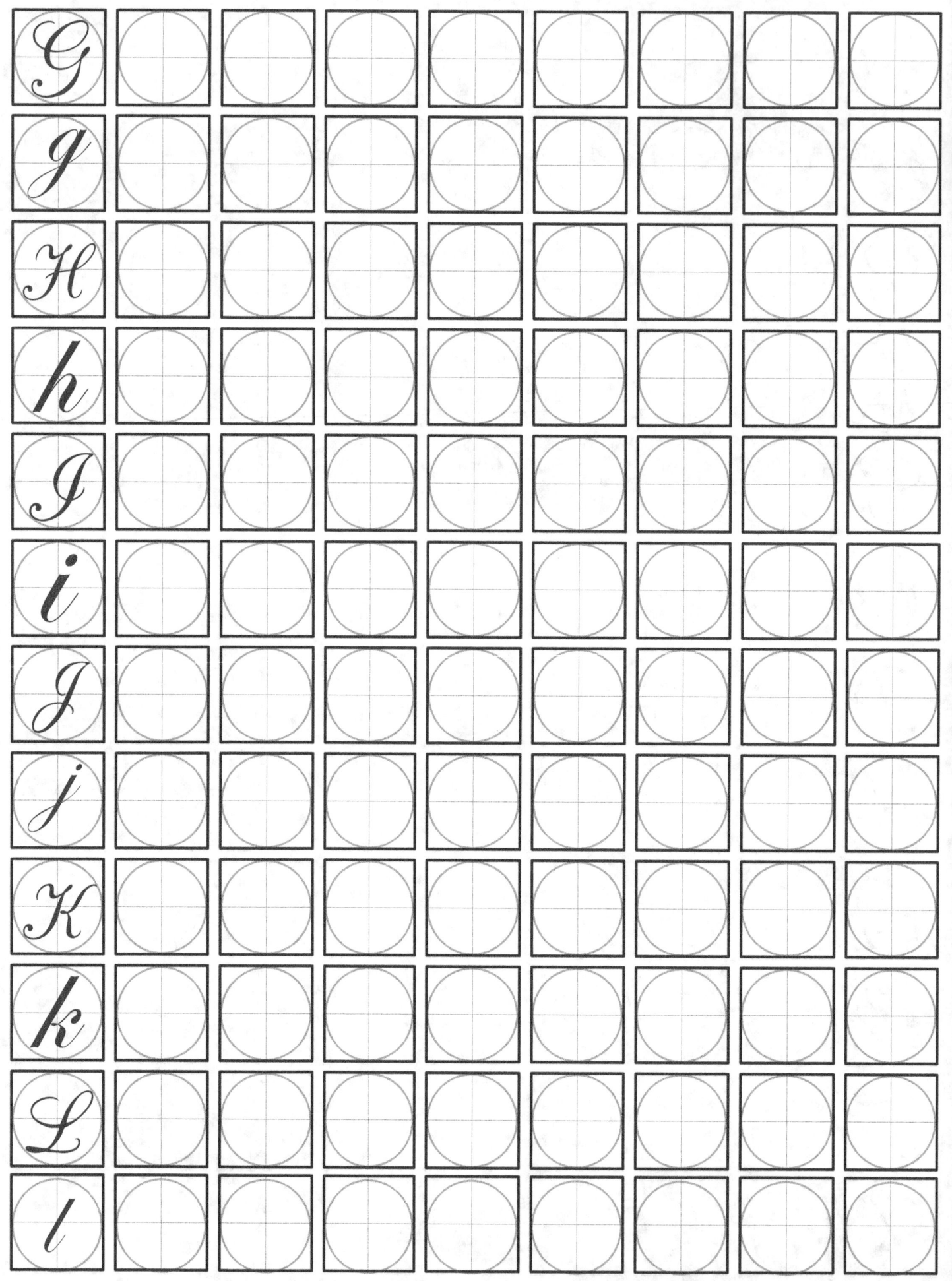

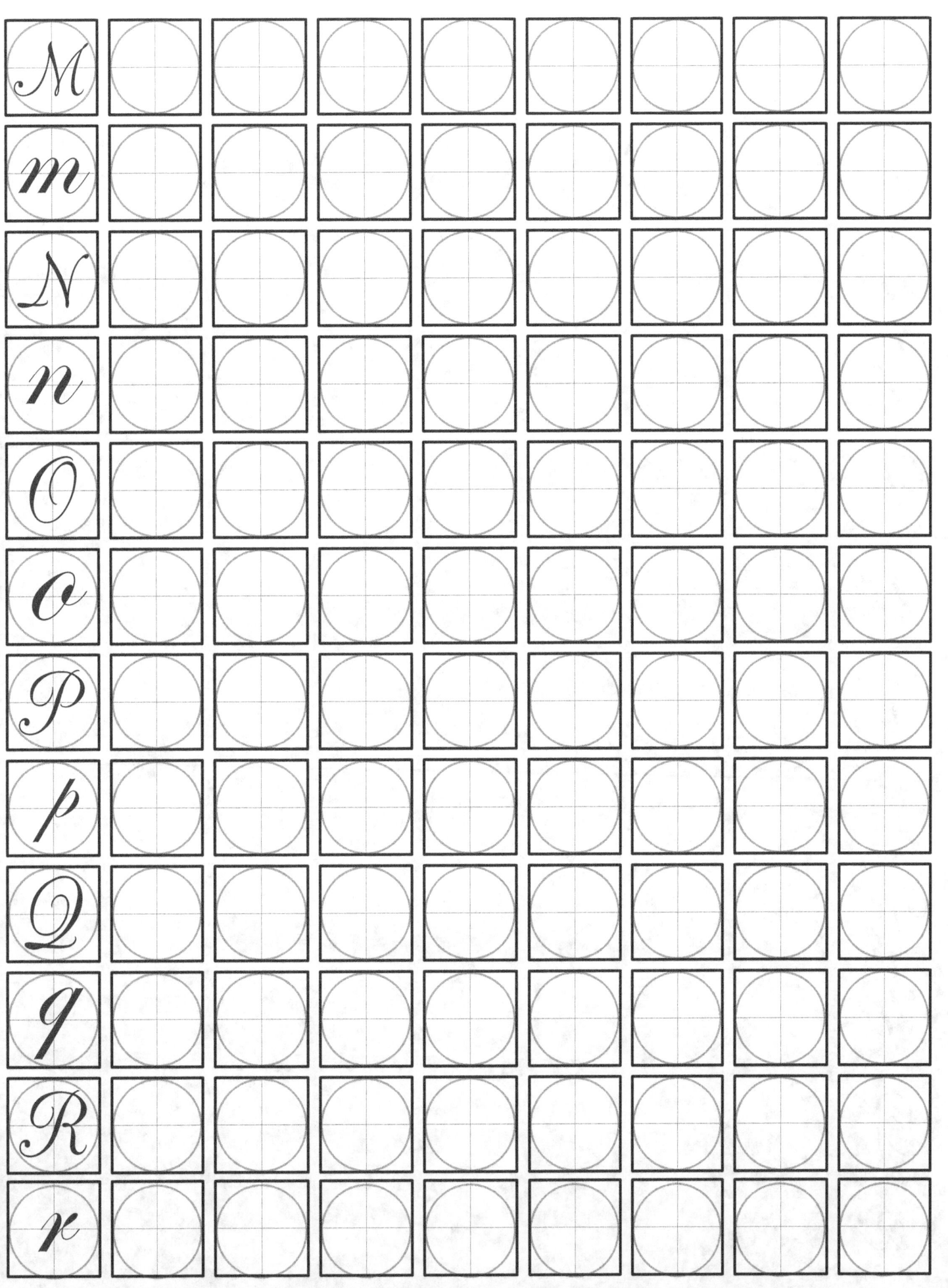

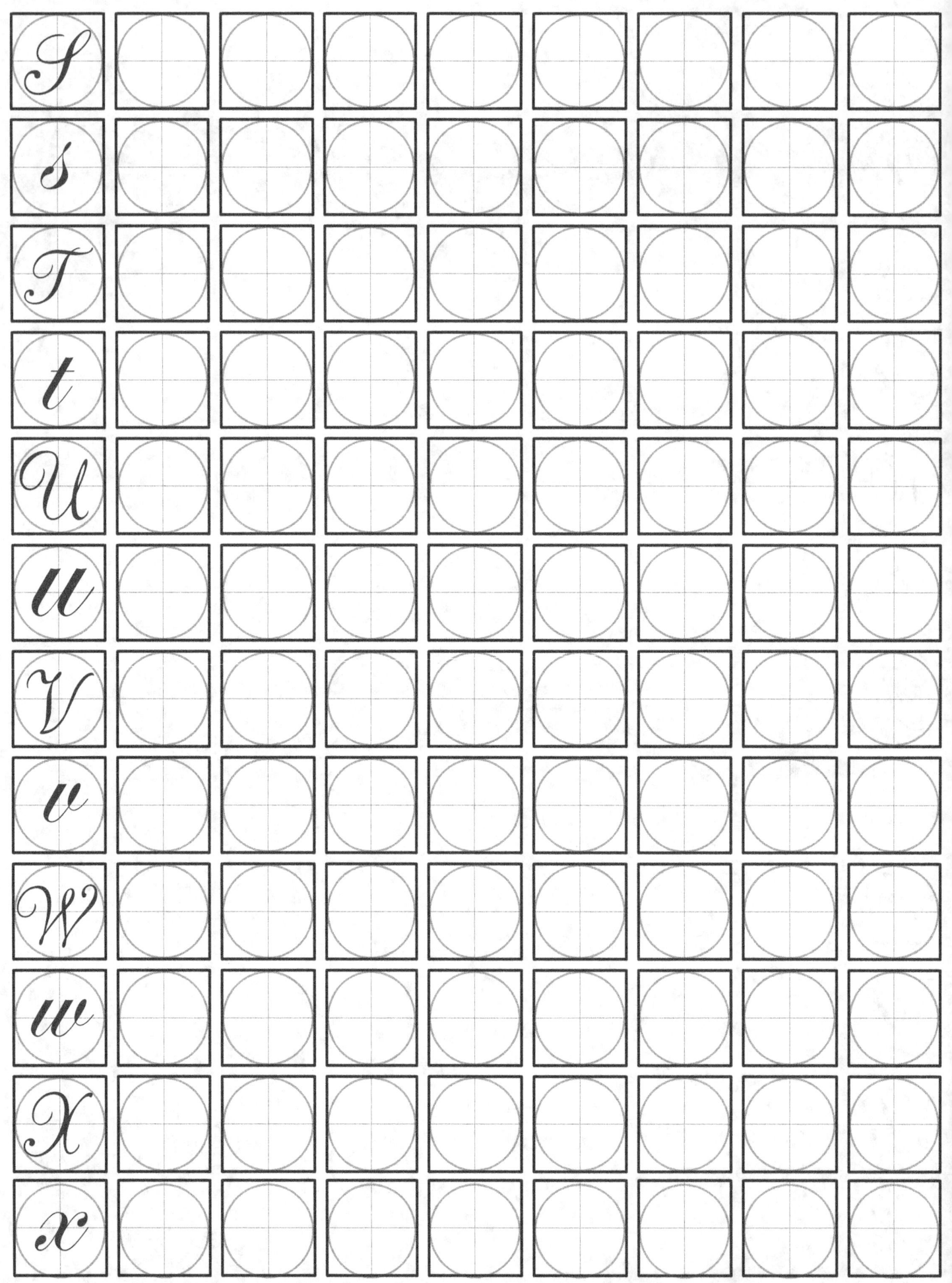

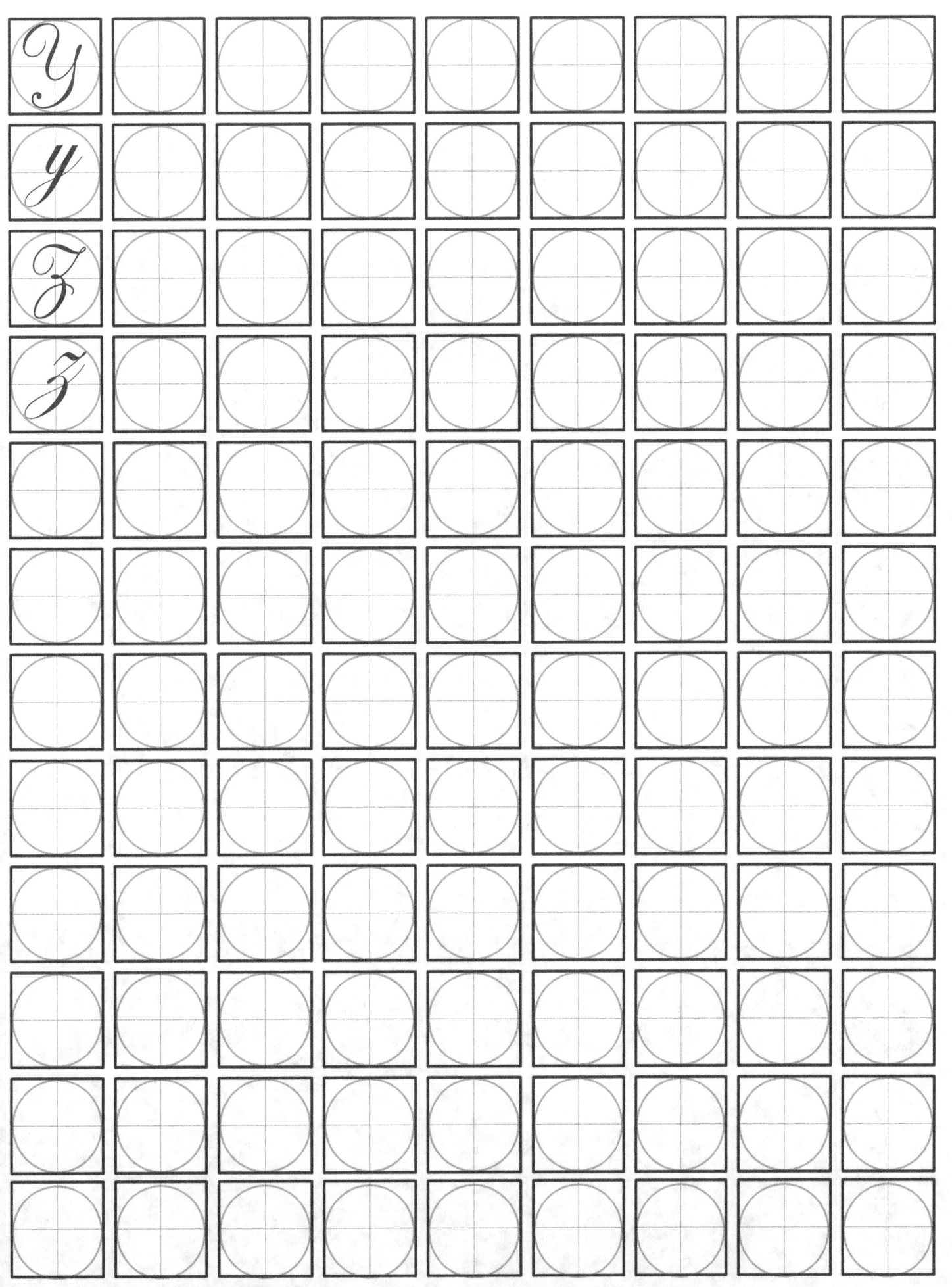

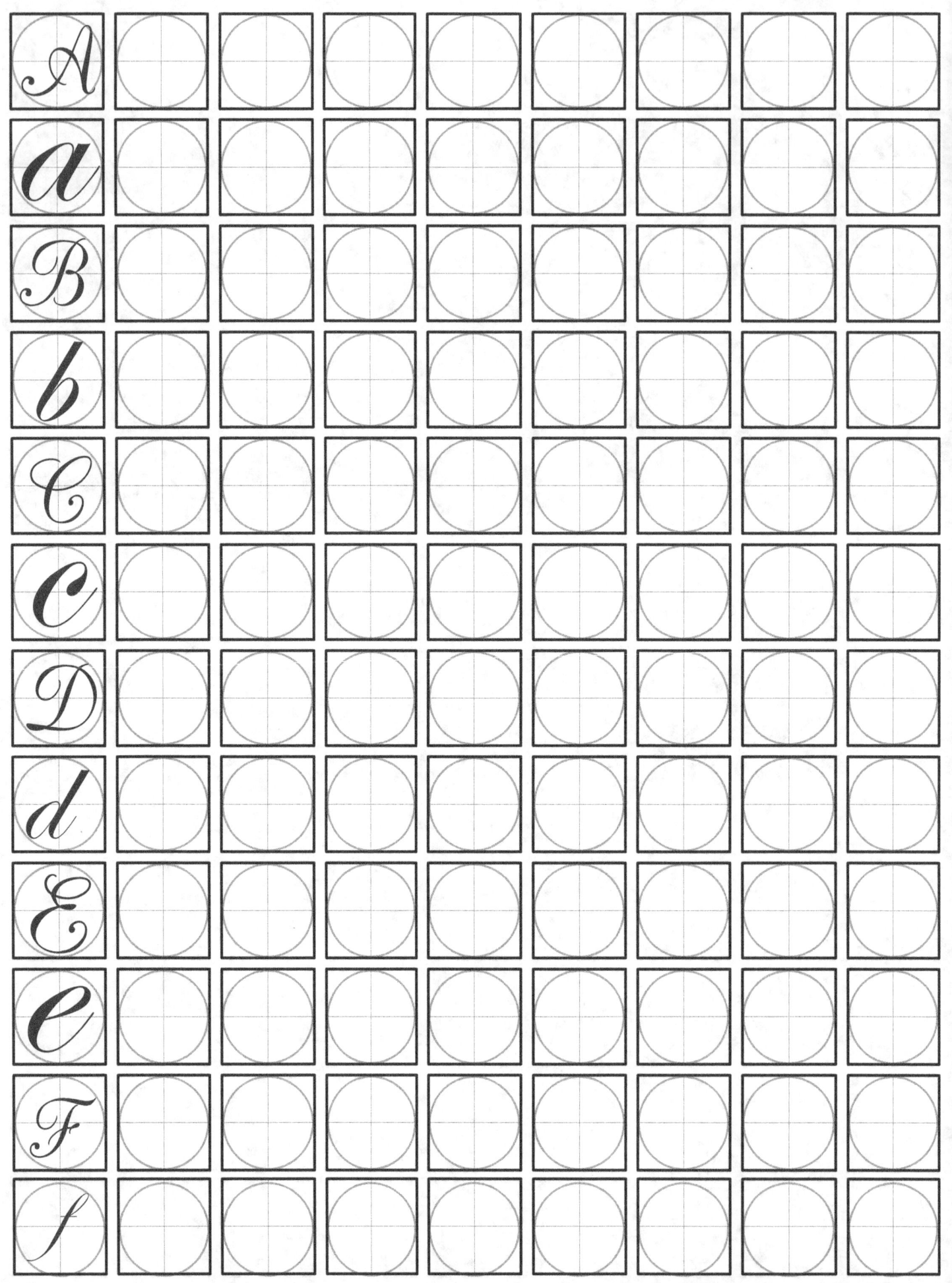

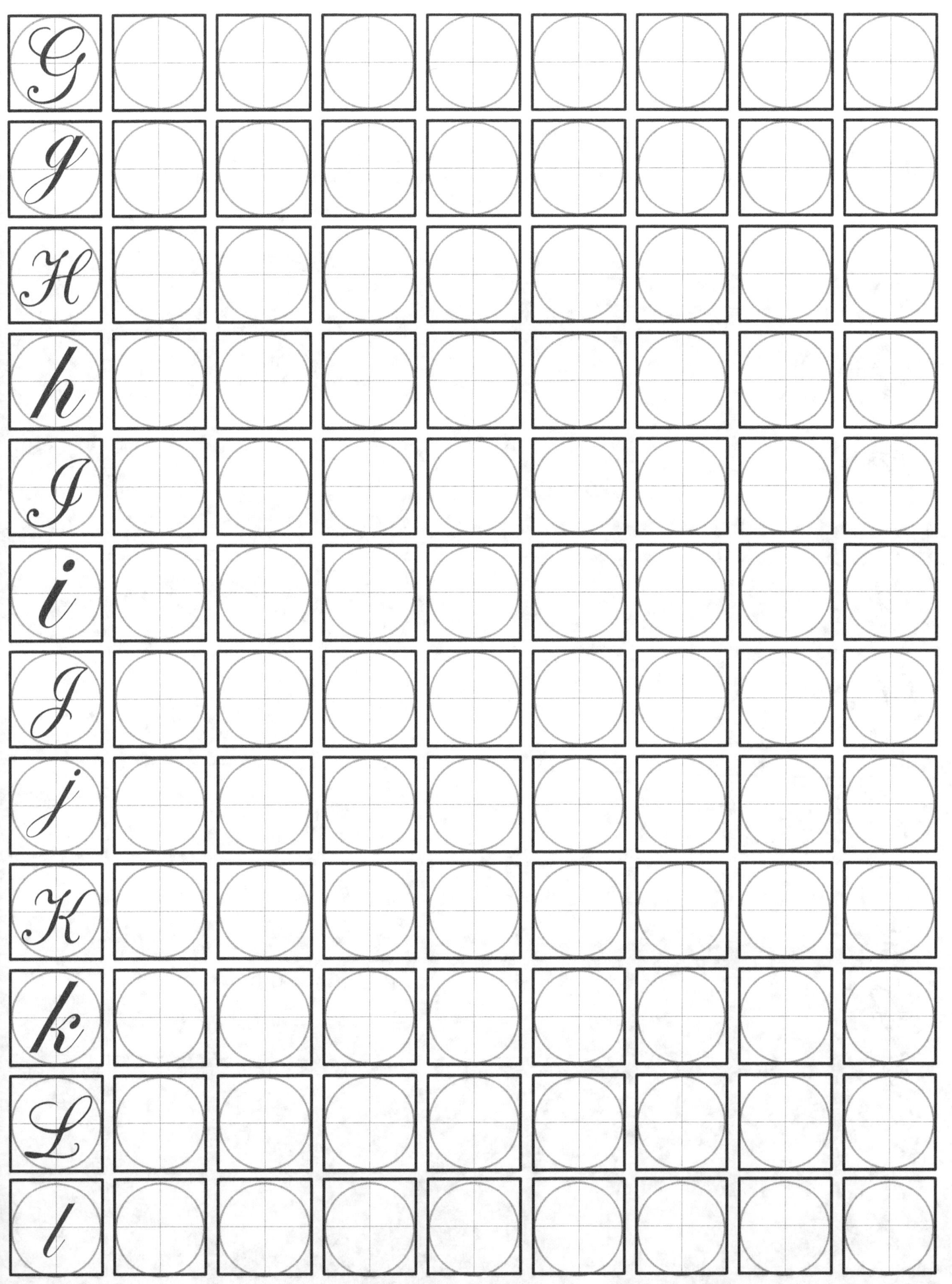

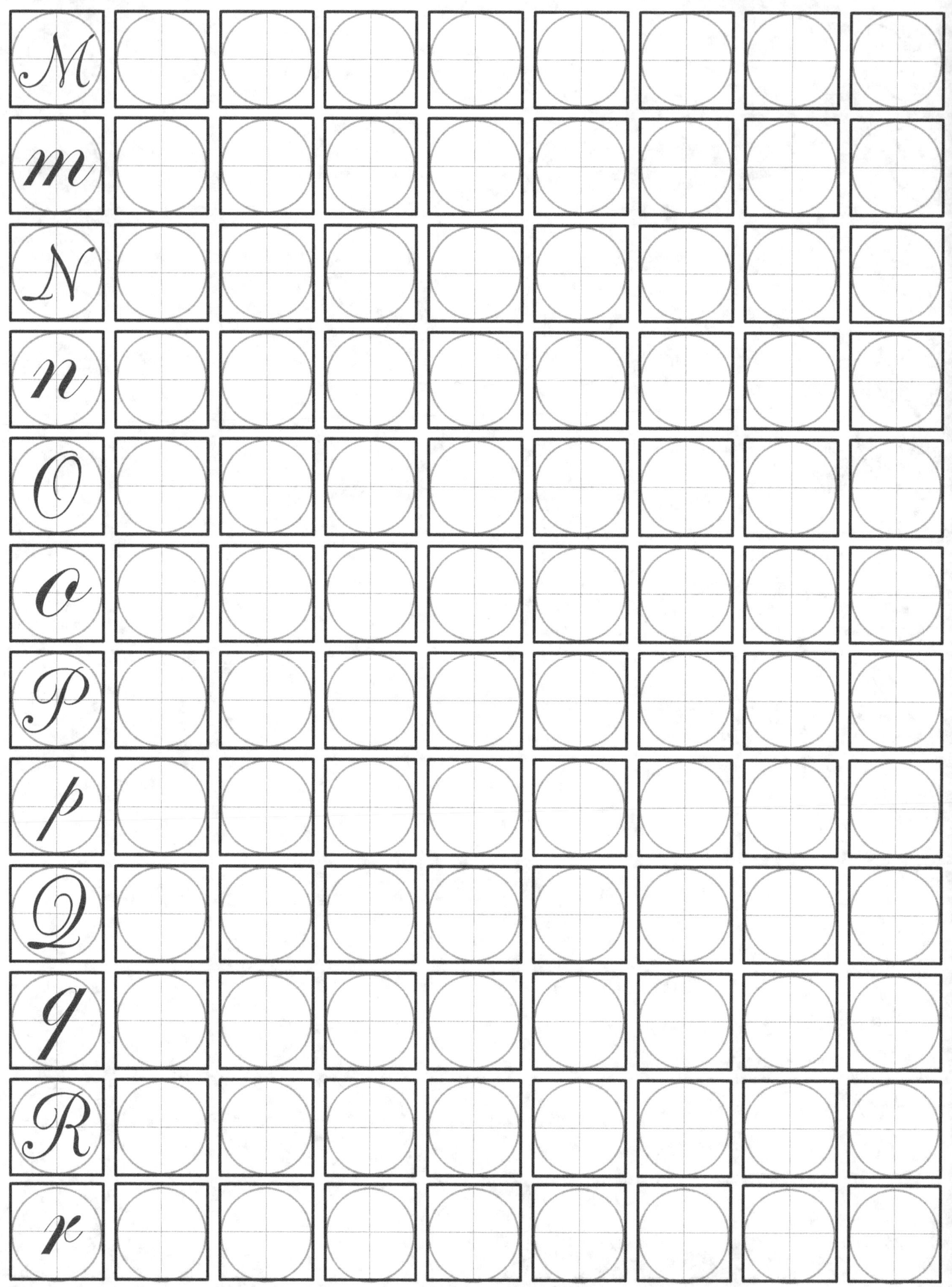

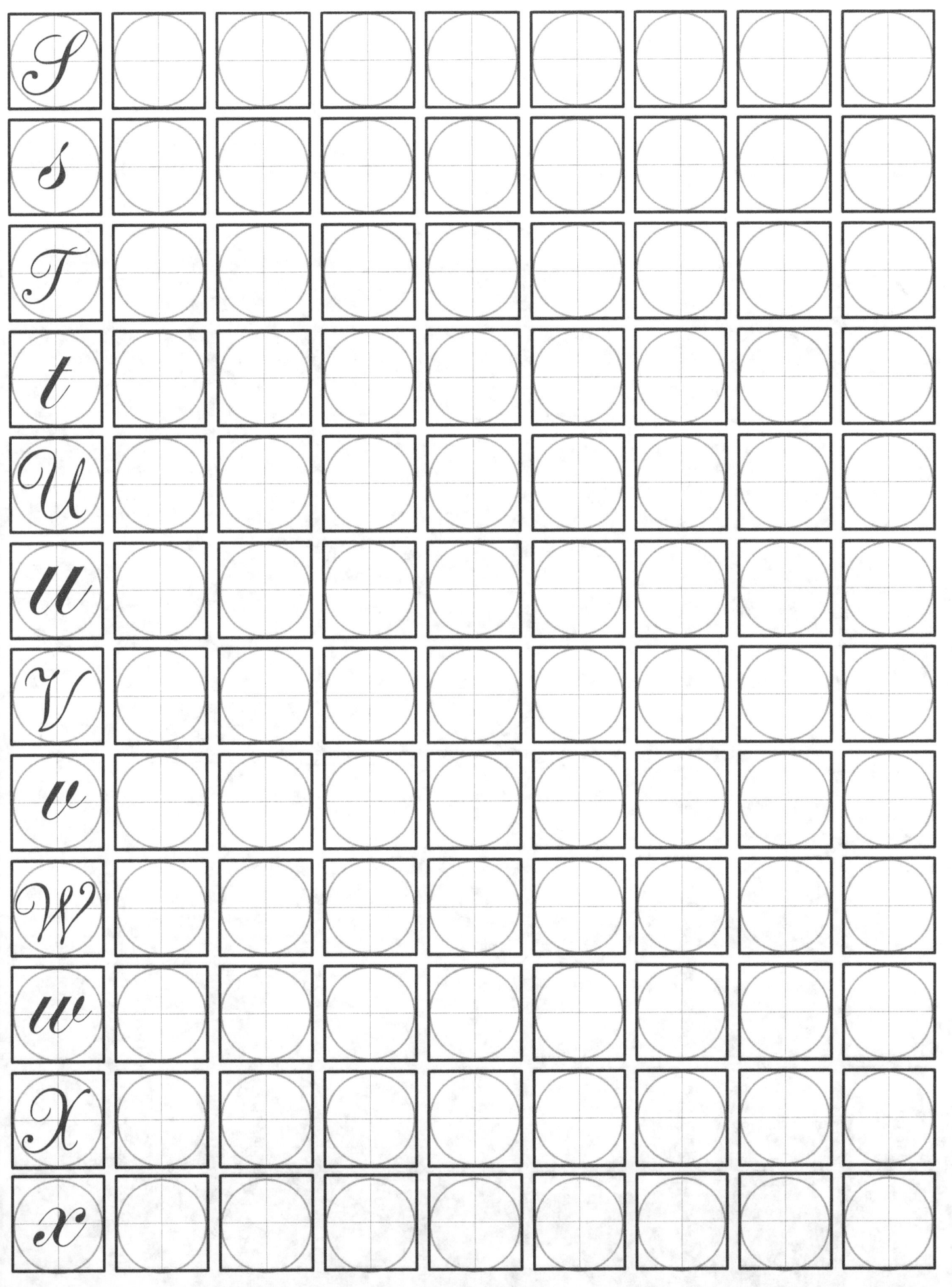

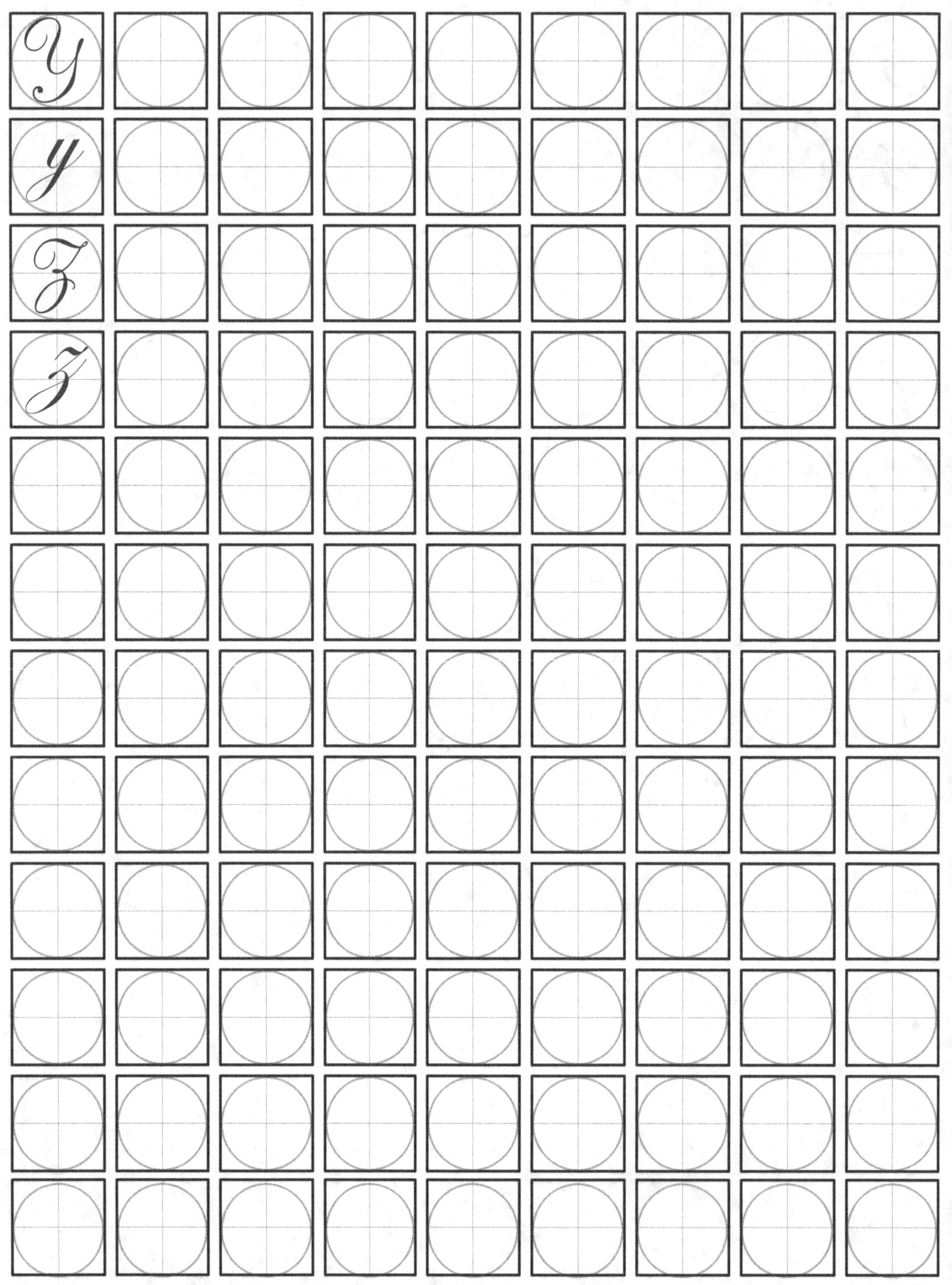

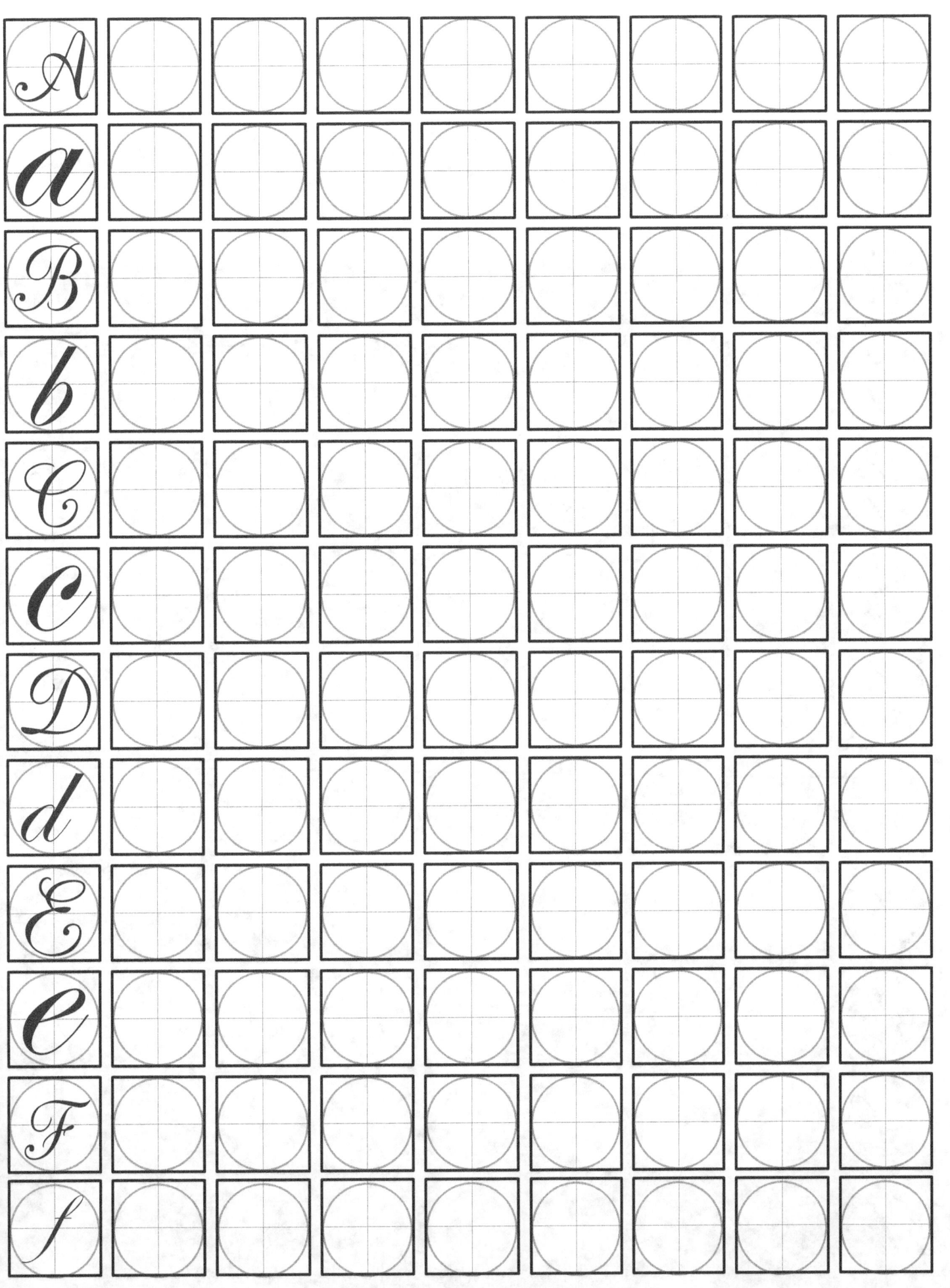

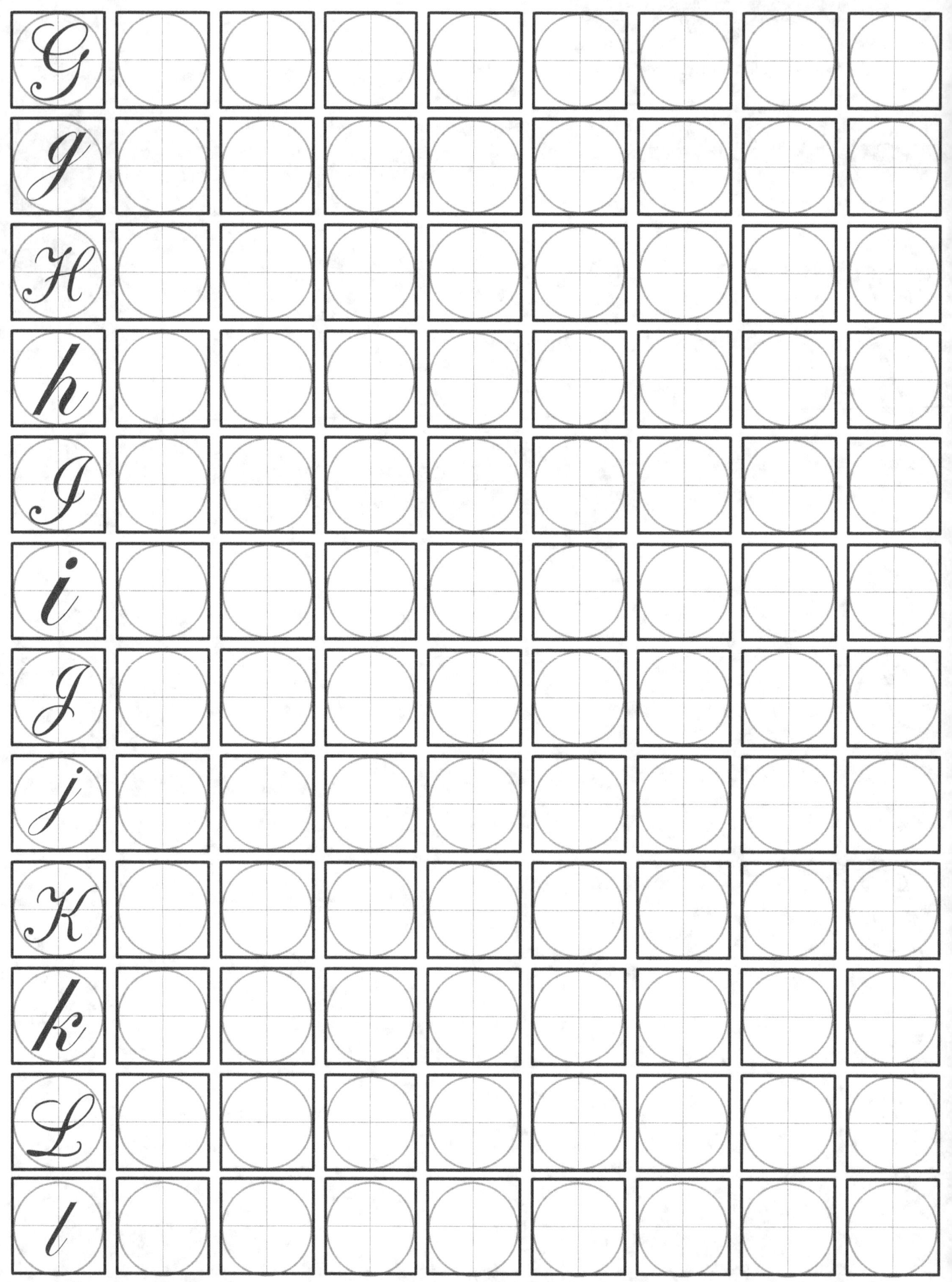

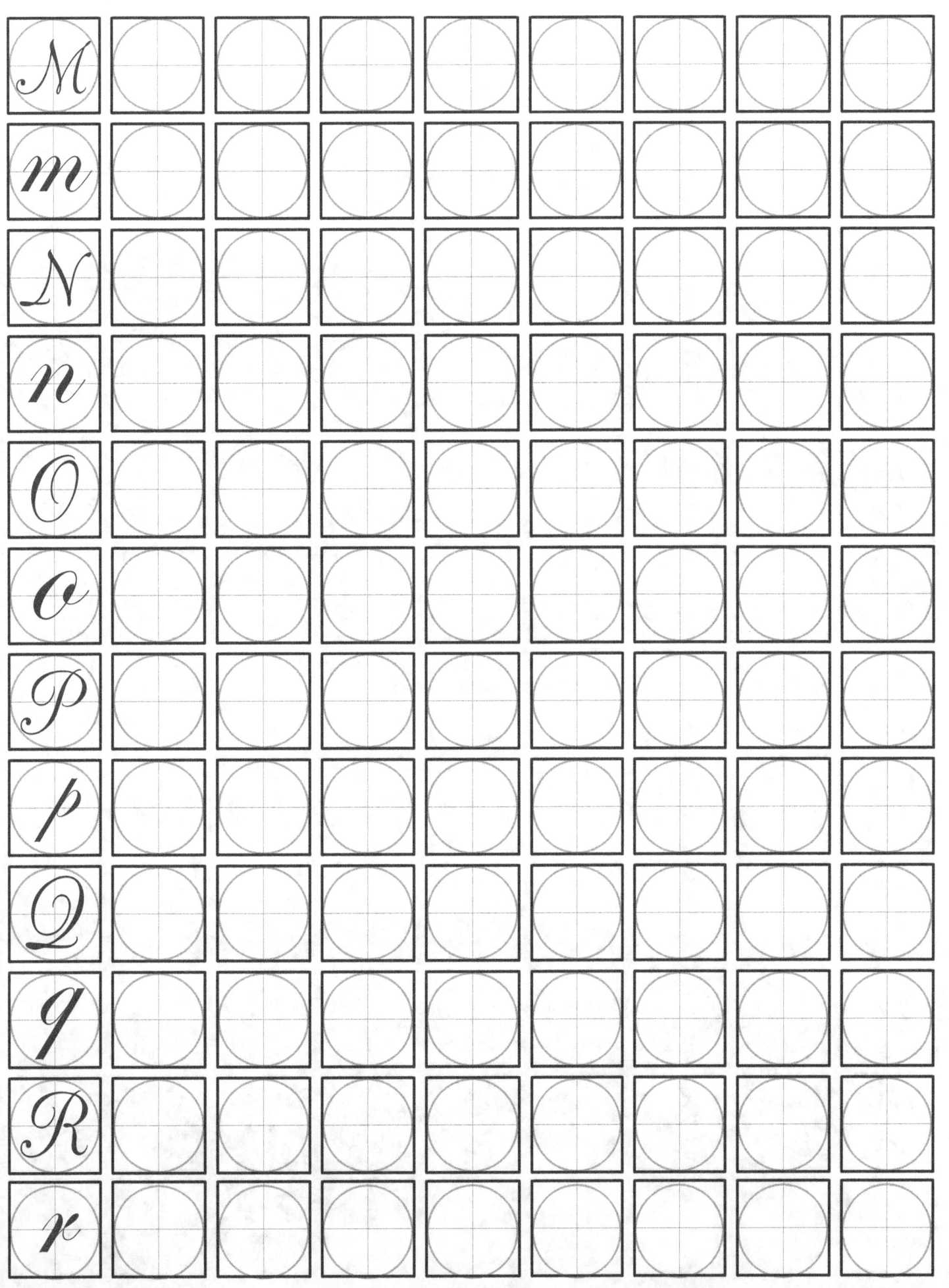

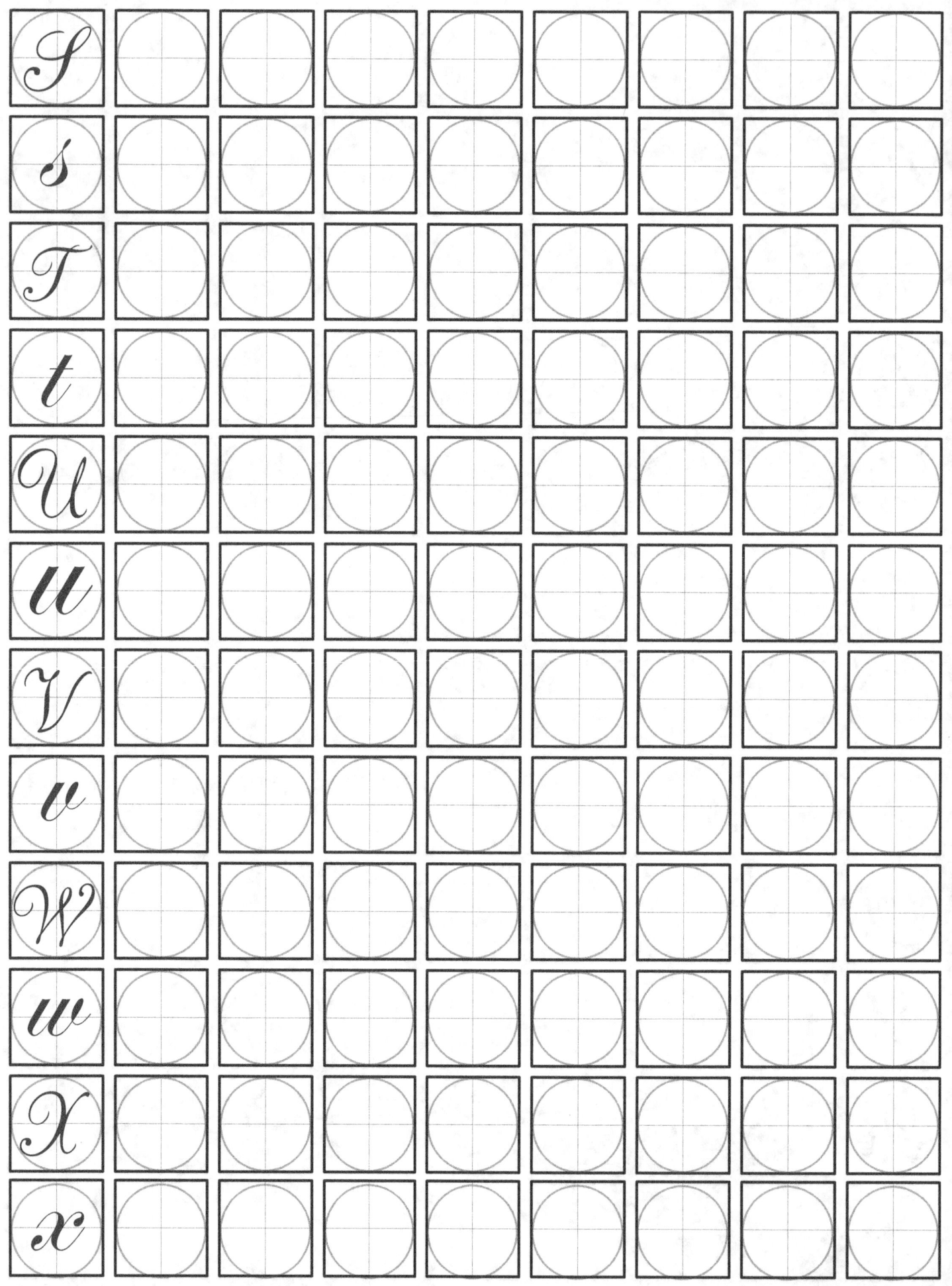

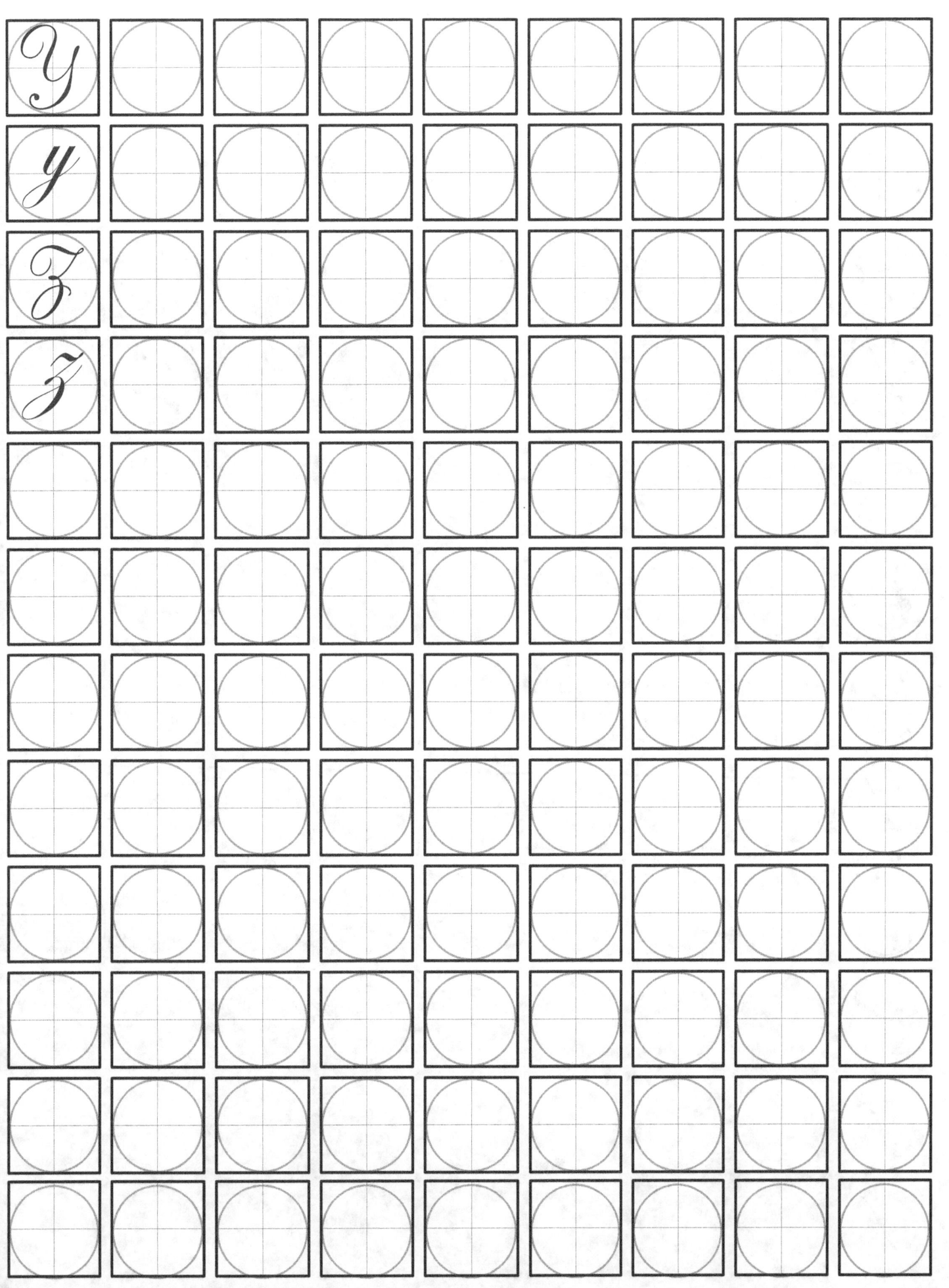

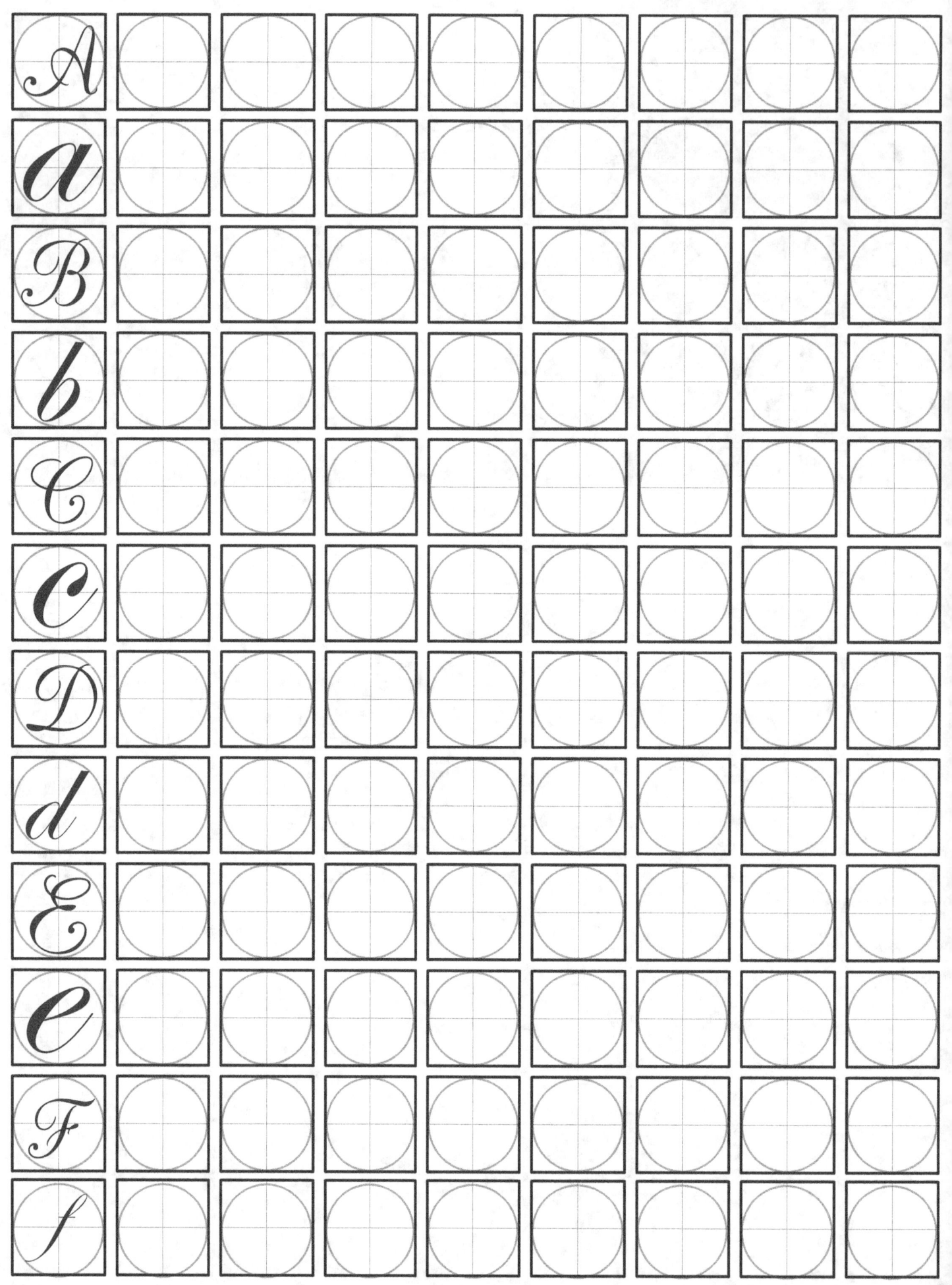

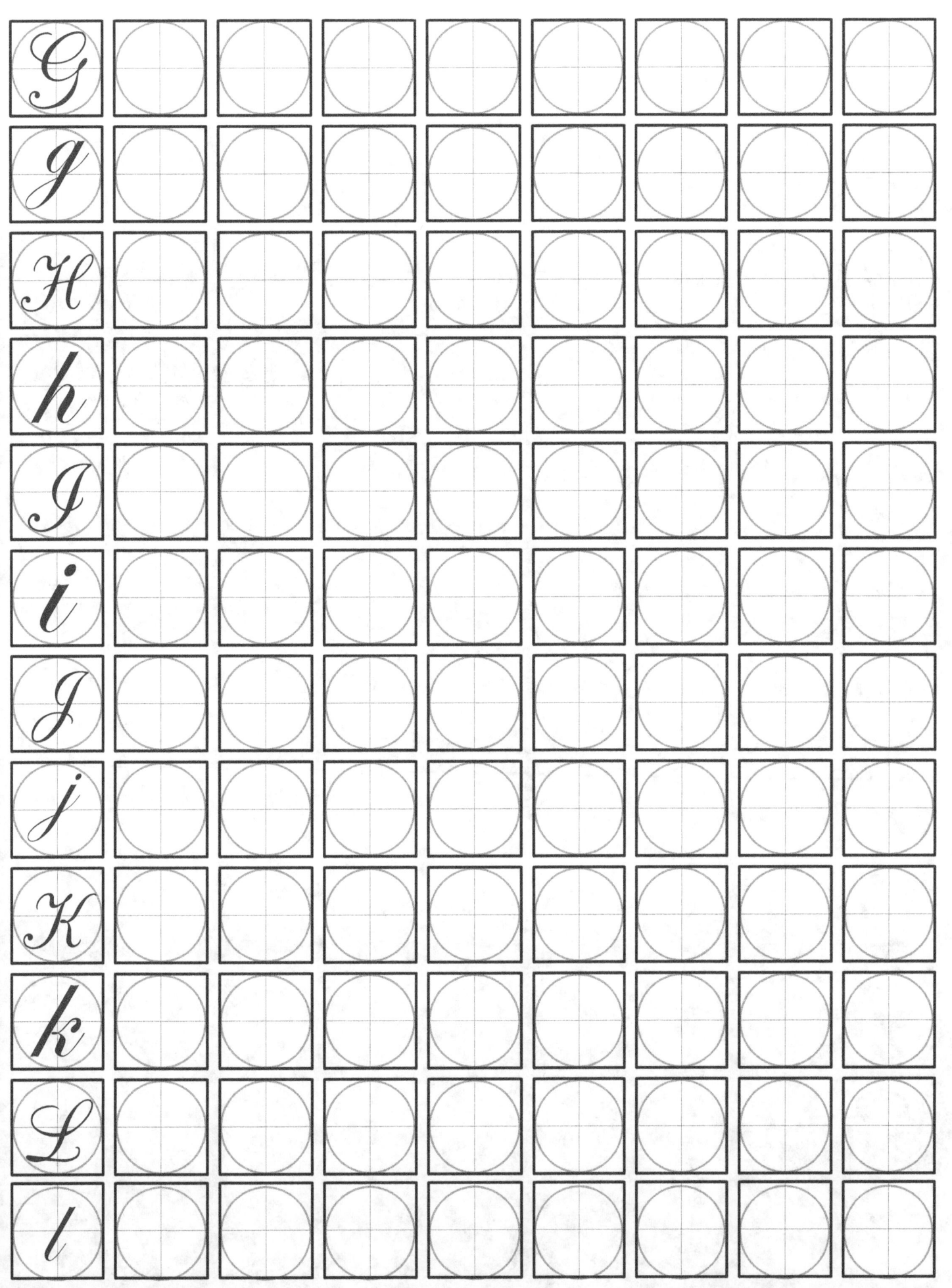

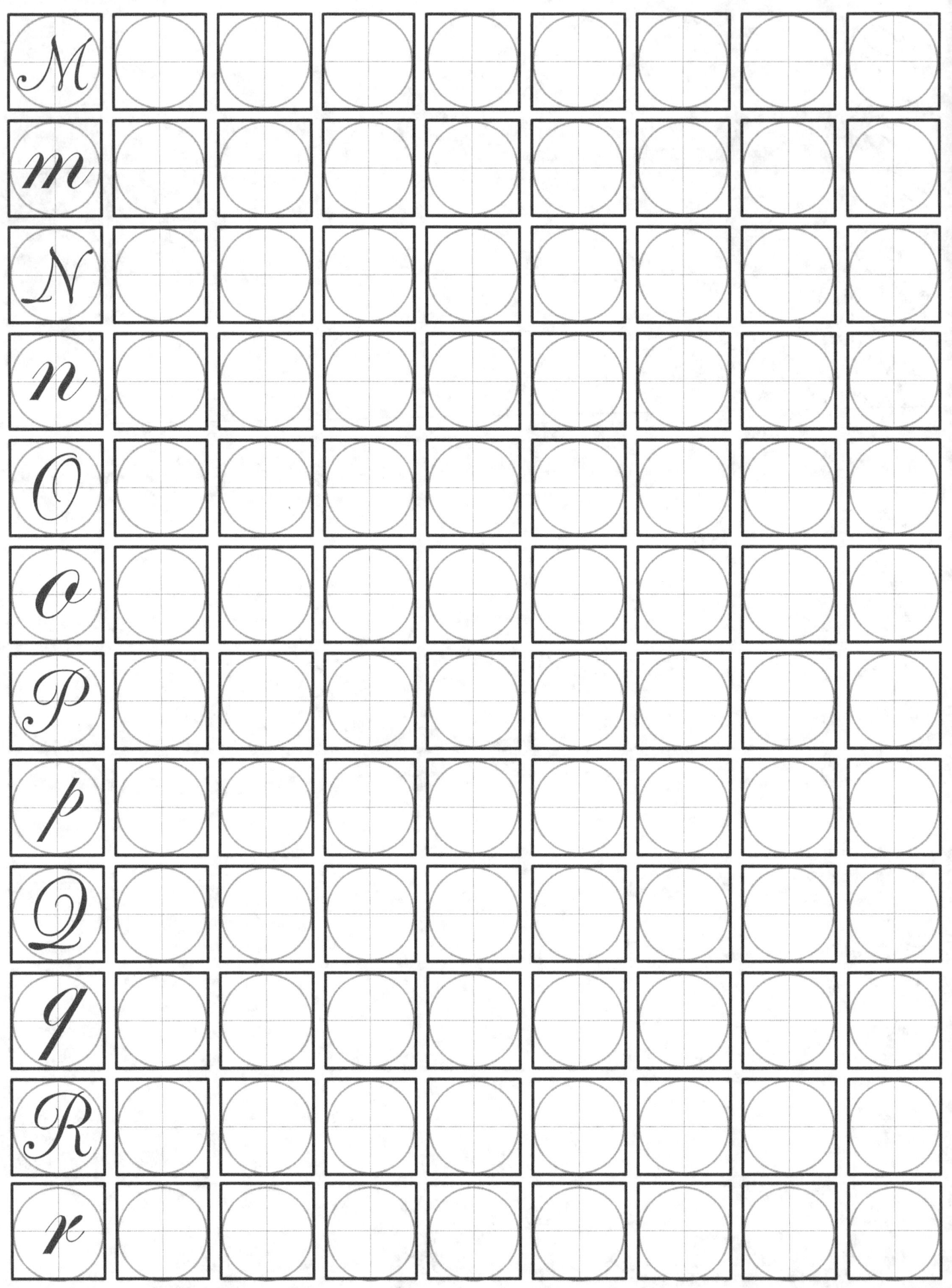

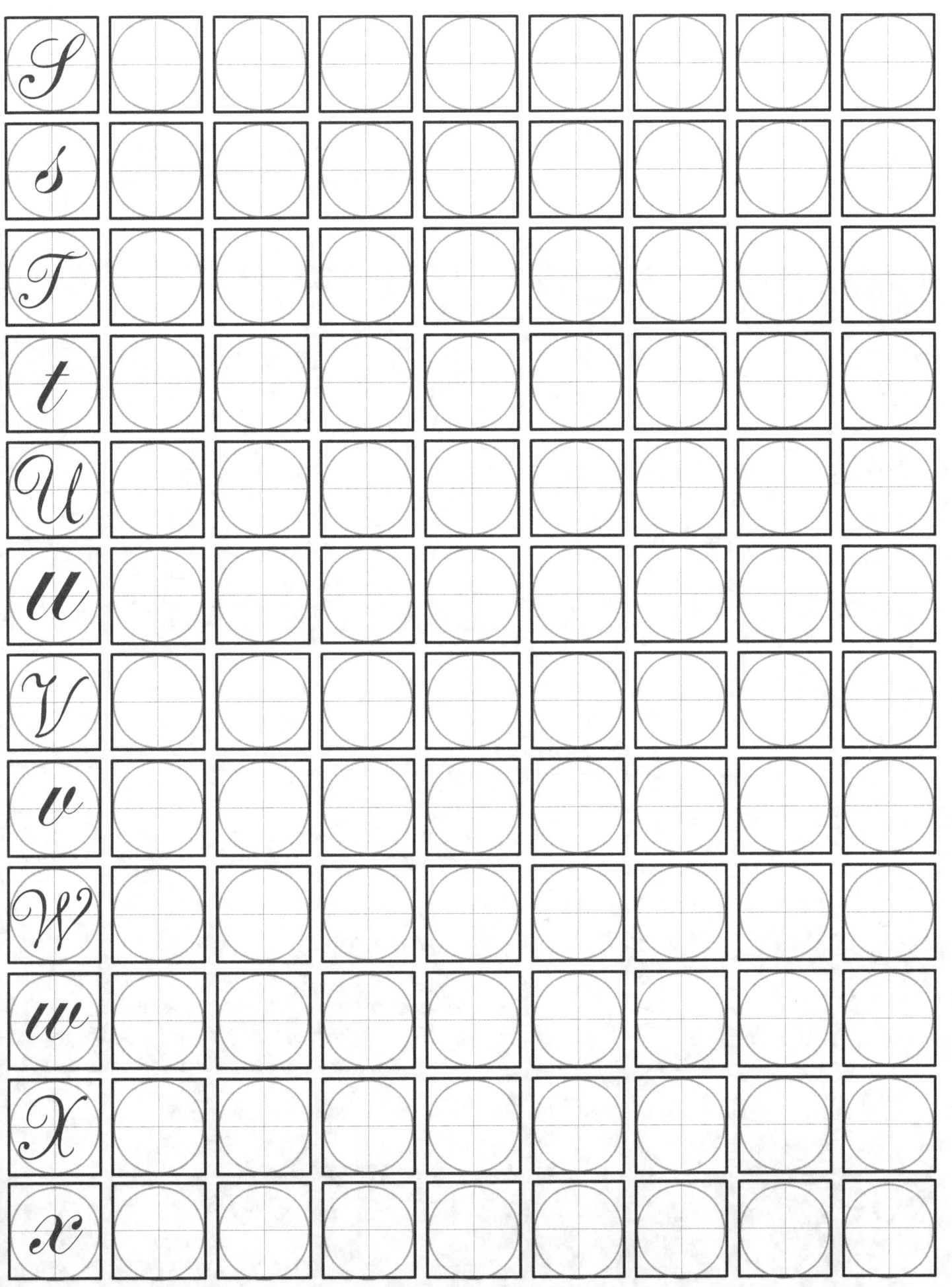

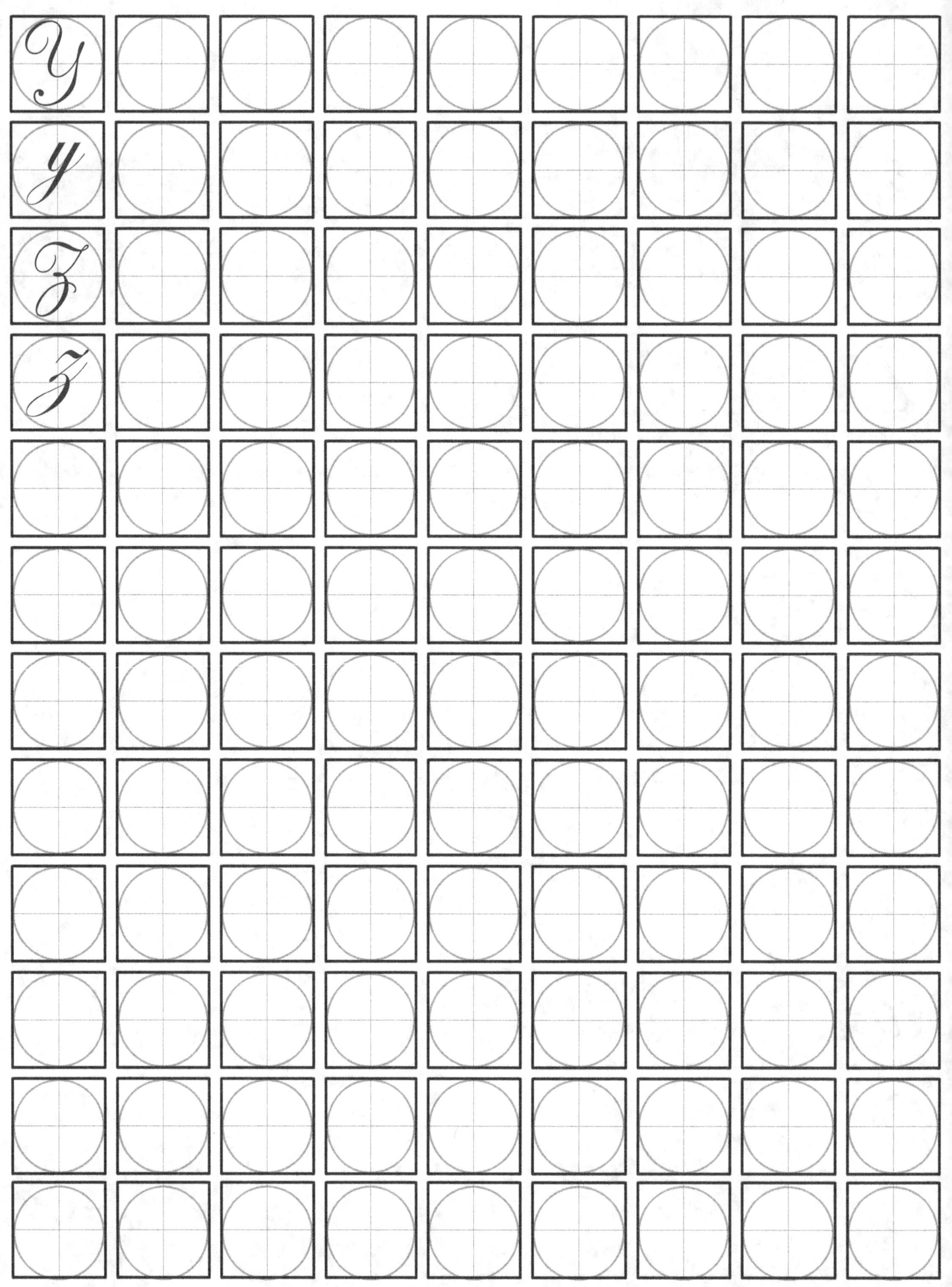

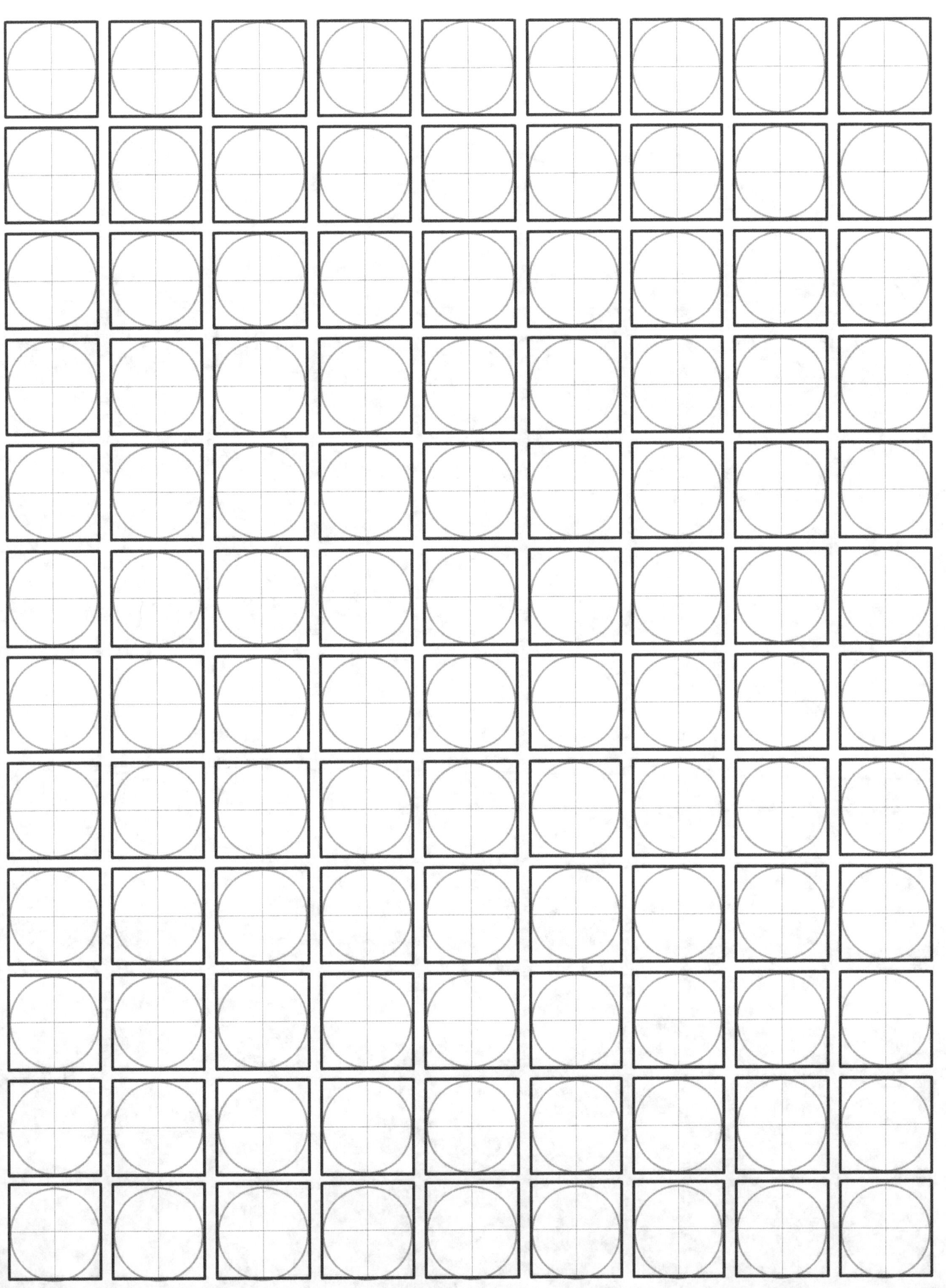

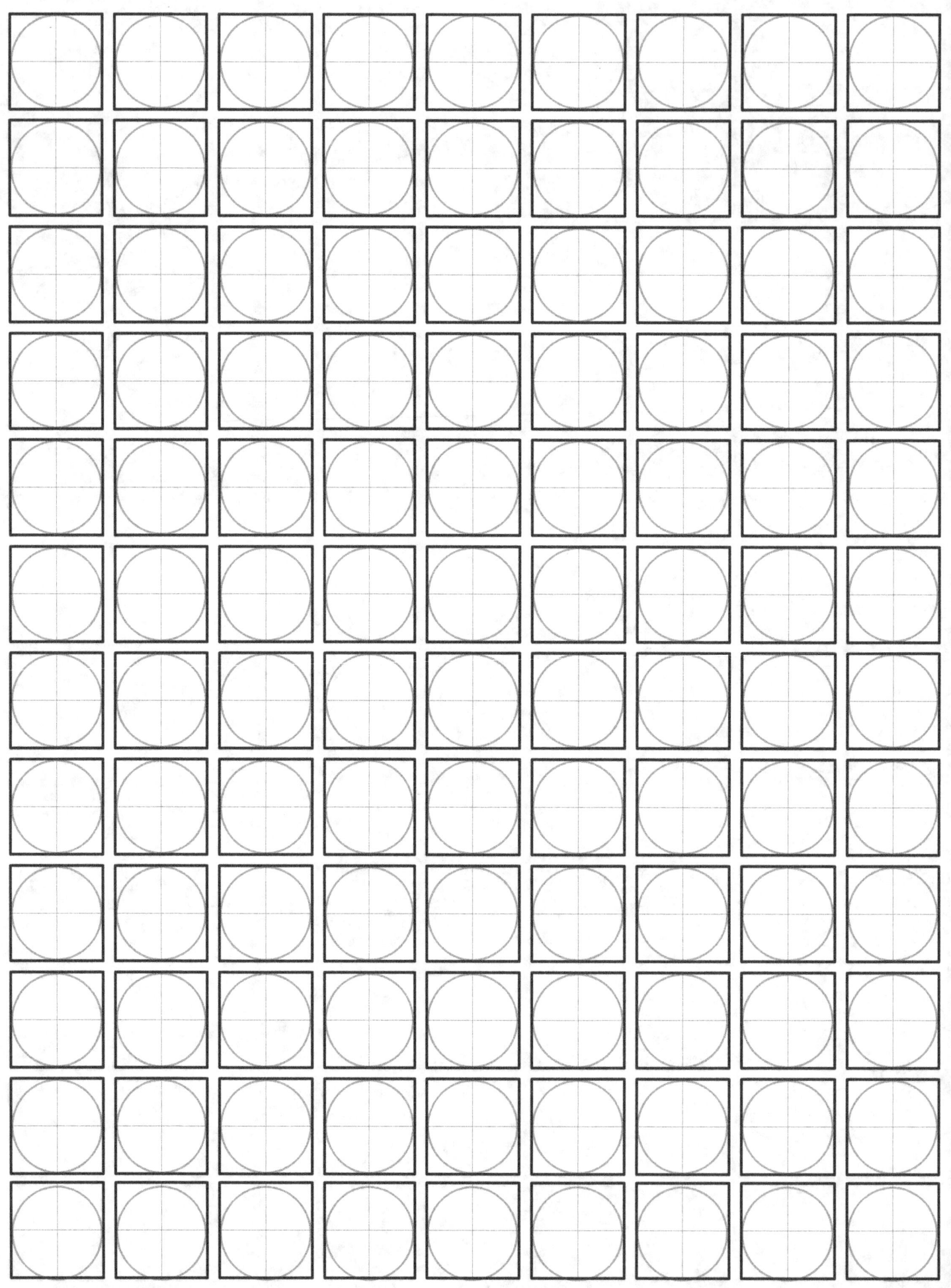

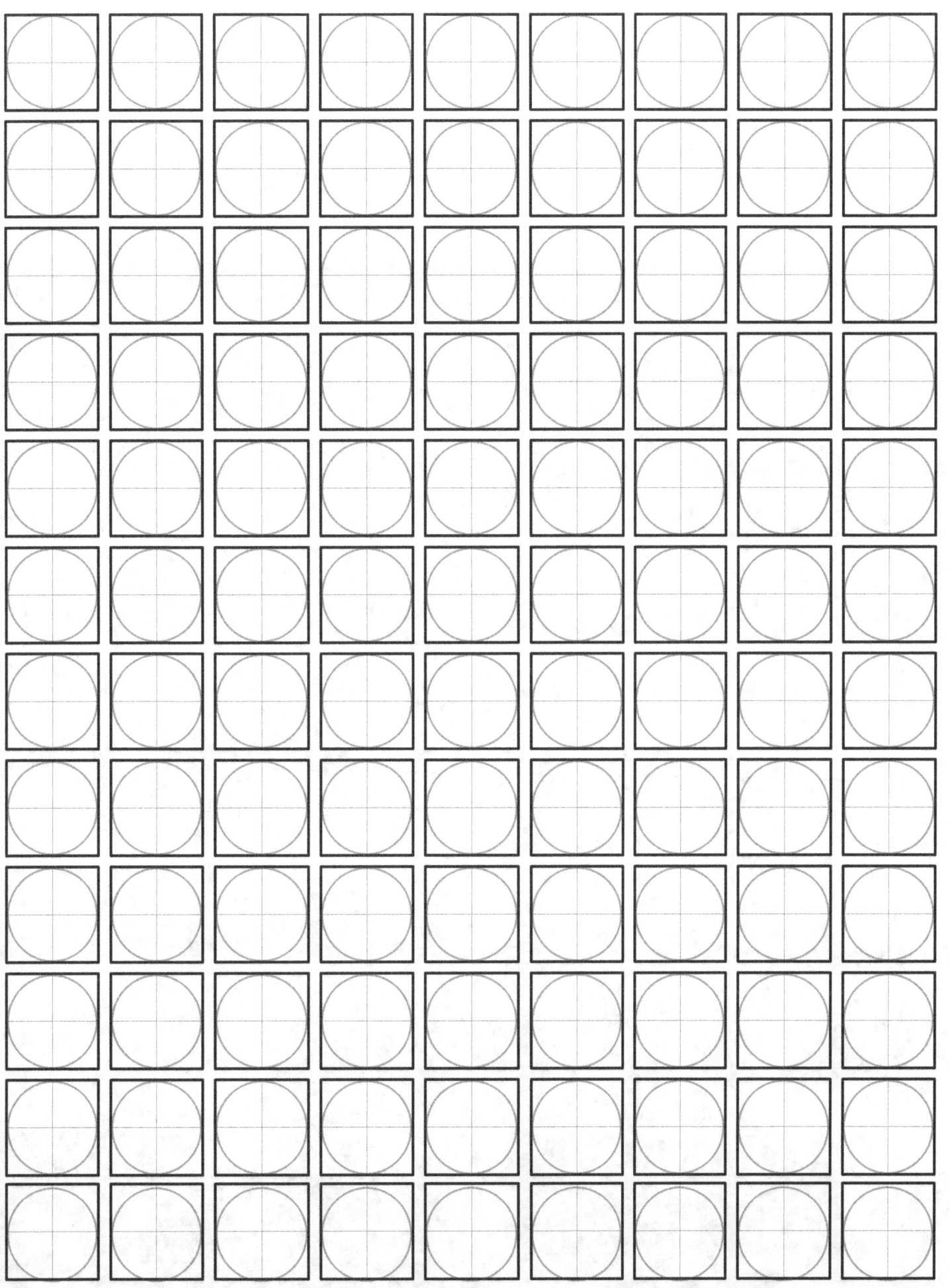

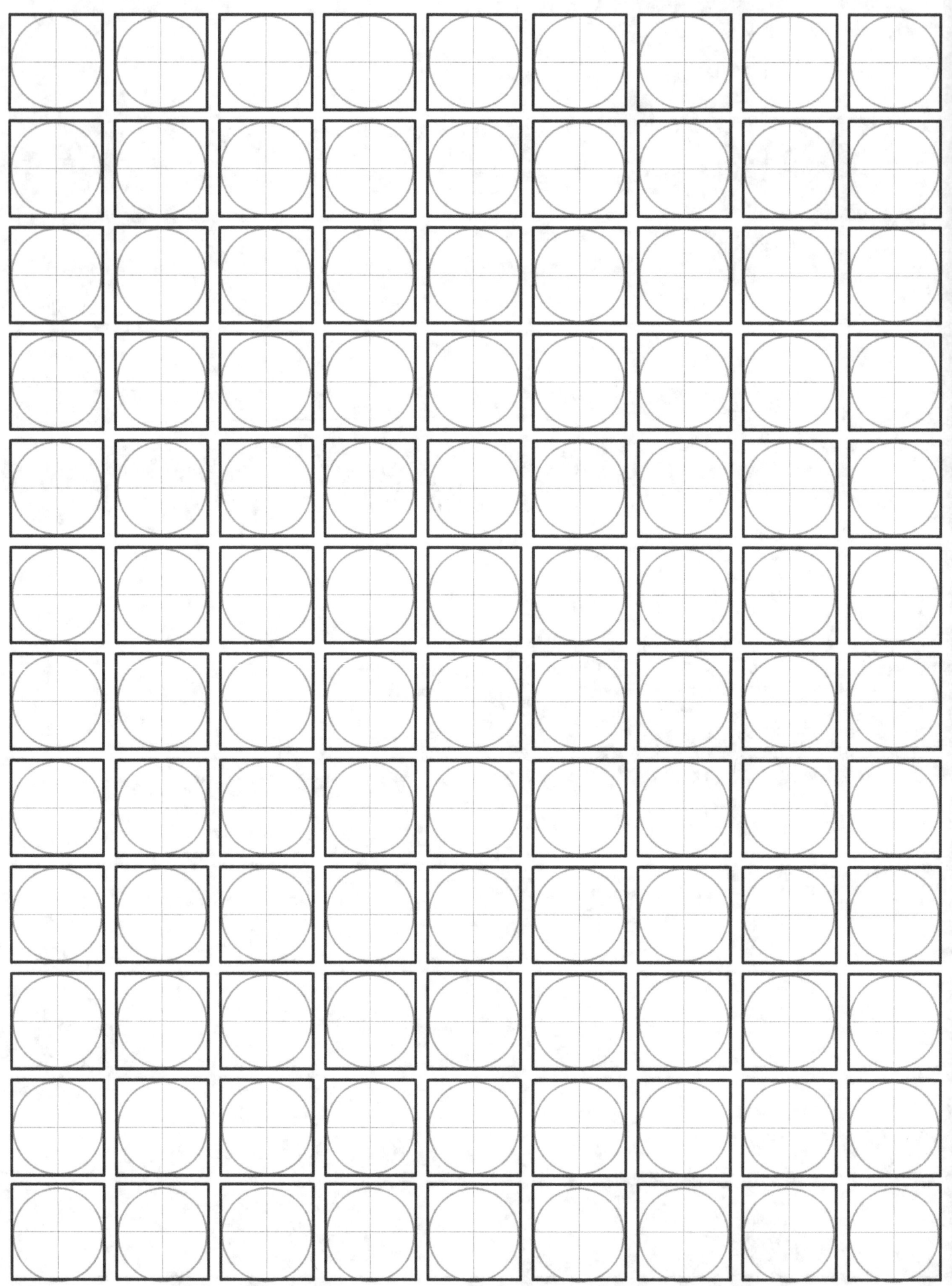

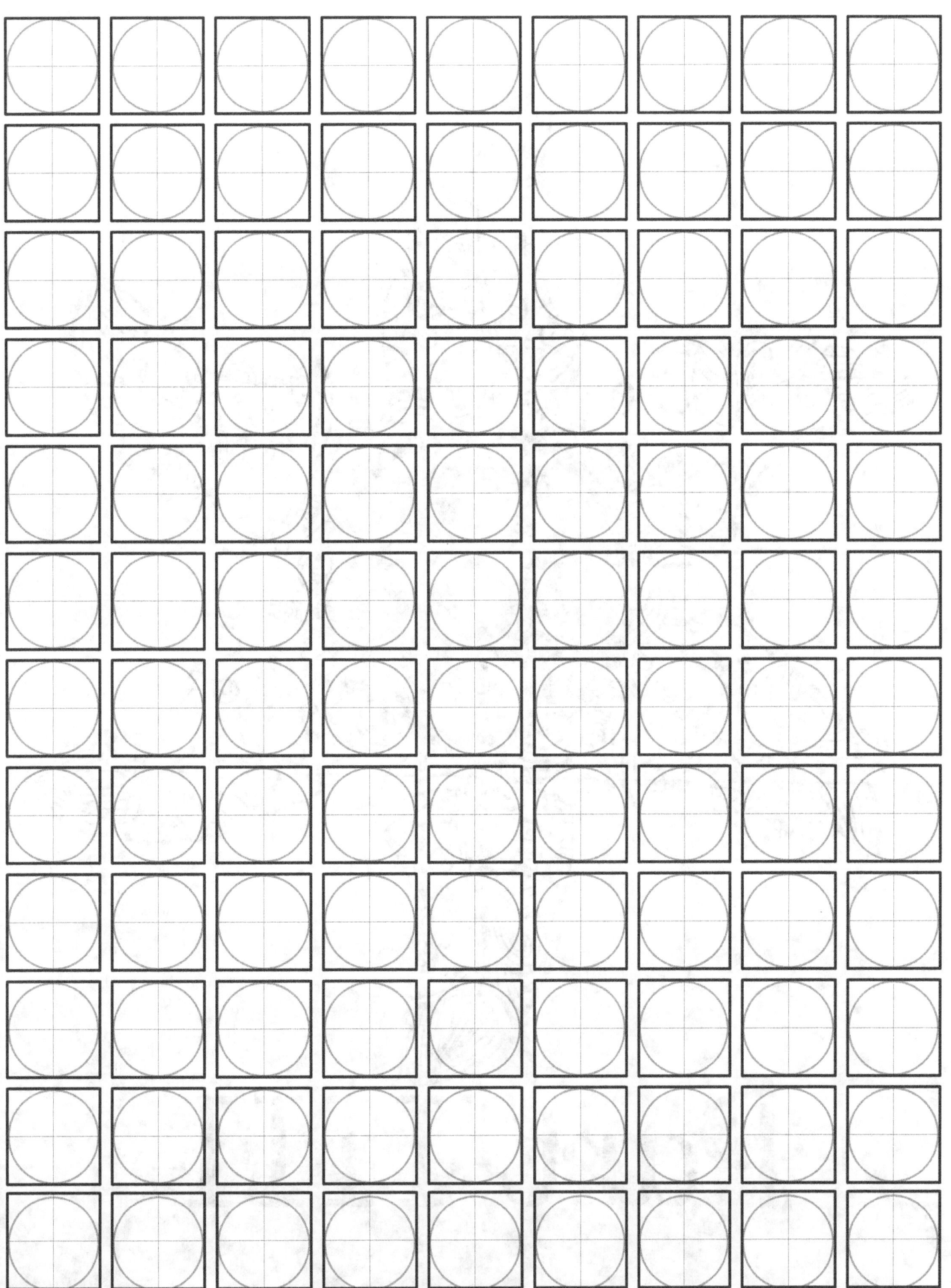

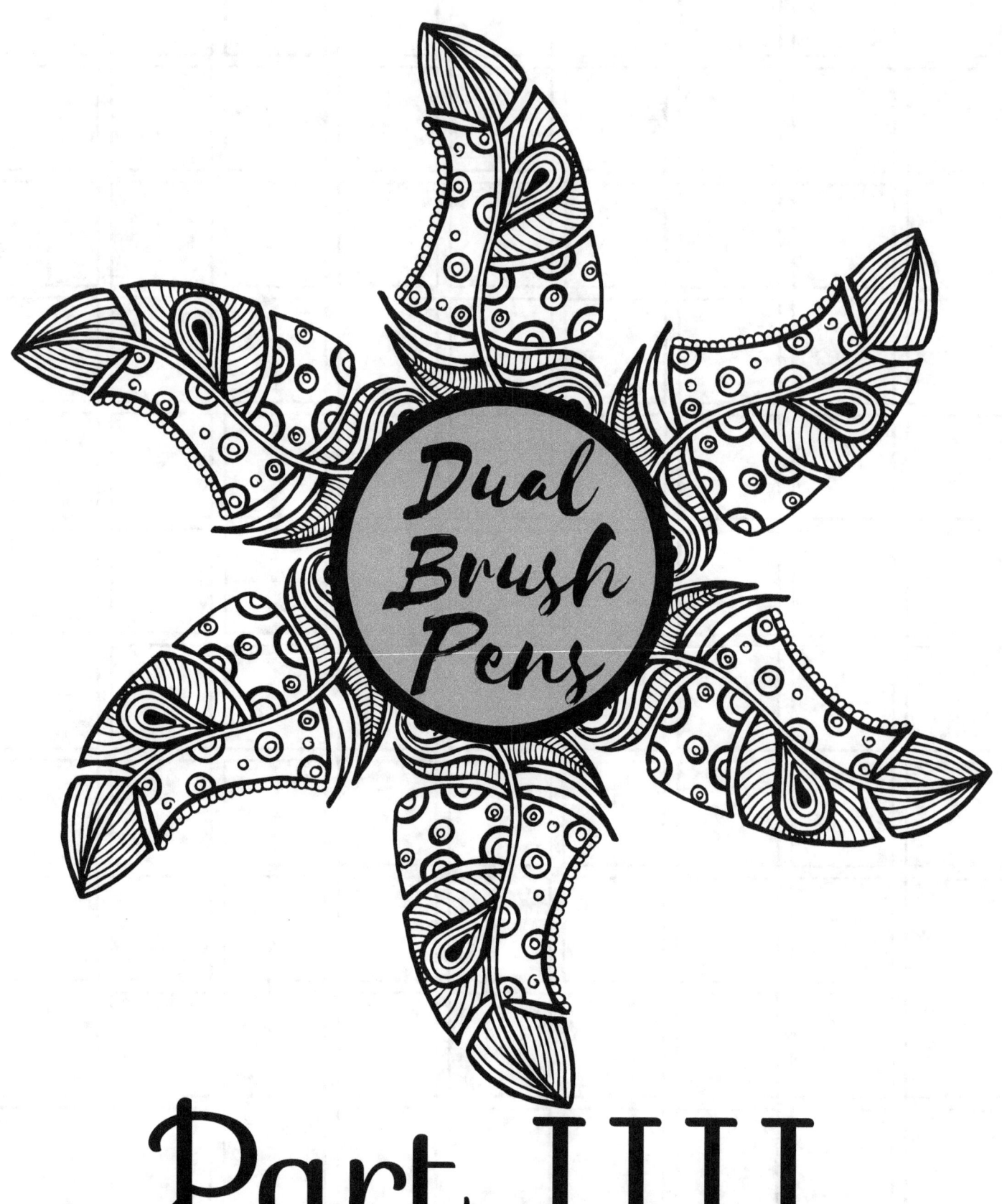

Part IIII

DUAL BRUSH PENS

DUAL BRUSH PENS

DUAL BRUSH PENS

DUAL BRUSH PENS

DUAL BRUSH PENS

DUAL BRUSH PENS

DUAL BRUSH PENS

DUAL BRUSH PENS

DUAL BRUSH PENS

DUAL BRUSH PENS

DUAL BRUSH PENS

DUAL BRUSH PENS

DUAL BRUSH PENS

DUAL BRUSH PENS

www.ingramcontent.com/pod-product-compliance
Lightning Source LLC
Chambersburg PA
CBHW081735220526
45468CB00008B/2109